TAVEL
The People and the Wines

© 2011 Éditions Féret, Bordeaux
Translation by Josephine Bacon, Tamr Translations Limited, London, UK
ISBN: 978-2-35156-094-5

Rolf Bichsel

TRANSLATION BY JOSEPHINE BACON

Tavel
THE PEOPLE
AND THE WINES

FÉRET

Acknowledgements

This book would never have come into existence without the support of a number of people. First of all, I must thank all the grape-growers of Tavel and their enthusiastic president Richard Maby. All of them welcomed me with the greatest kindness, putting all their trust in me without attempting to influence me in any way. They opened the doors of their cellars to me, as well as their hearts and transformed themselves into photographic models with the greatest of patience during the long photographic sessions whose only purpose was to show them as they really are. I should also like to thank Monsieur Thérond, the Mayor of Tavel, who allowed me free access to his parlour, enabling me to study valuable documents. He transformed himself into a talented communicator talent and enabled me to familiarise myself with Tavel as it is today. I must also thank Jacques Maby and Jacques Reboul for the research they performed into the local geography and history, and I have quoted from them in the relevant places. I also express my gratitude to Fabrice Delorme who made geological and historical studies available to me that proved very useful. He telephoned me regularly to ensure that I had not forgotten anything or anyone. And finally thank you to Eric Pfifferling, who was able to convey to me his love and passion for genuine Tavel wine, to Sandrine for her hamburgers and fries served quickly and with a friendly smile, to Elisabeth for the delicious jams that helped me to start my day a boost – and everything else.

But this book could never have moved from the clumsy embryonic stage to a serious volume without the assistance of two delightful and loyal ladies whom I thank most particularly. They are Sandra Gay, who never counted the hours or skimped in her efforts to arrange my stay, to accompany me, to help me, to support me with such talent and efficiency during my research and my on-site meetings and Marie-Hélène Mondary, who patiently reread, reviewed and corrected my French with vigilance, sensitivity and respect. I have made the language my own with the passion of a lover and the faith of a convert.

Rolf Bichsel

FORWARD

A book about Tavel? How come? This is the question I was asked by most of the local inhabitants on a virtually daily basis during those all-too-short weeks spent in the little village in the département of Gard. Had they asked for whom I was writing it, the reply would have been perfectly simple. I wanted to write and illustrate this book above all for my own pleasure, like a wine-maker who produces the wine he loves. The pleasure of conveying the richness of Tavel and of its wines in prose and images, to draw its varied forms and colours through words and photographs, to unfold this wonderful story of men and women talking about their native soil and what it means to them.

The why takes a little longer to explain but it is just as egotistic. In the current overloaded and overexploited world of media in which everything has been said or written, Tavel remains a unique and rare case in the history and culture of wine, a favourite subject for a chronicler such as myself. The village of Tavel is a sort of closed vessel separated from the rest of the world by an autoroute that seems to serve as a sort of Hadrian's Wall, protecting this benevolent civilisation from the unlettered barbarians. But on which side does the civilised world lie and on which barbarism?

After traversing the little tunnel under the autoroute that leads to the village, plunging head first into a sort of time door, the visitor who is rather shaken by the experience uncovers at the other end of the tunnel a rather small area, probably a little outdated, through which runs a narrow départemental road. Let us not be fooled by appearances! The world indeed exists beyond Tavel, the village is merely a throughway, a decisive stage on the route to initiation. Although the départemental road is always filled with vans, tractors, school buses, Belgian 4x4s and scooters ridden by the youth of Tavel, everything (still) seems to be curiously well preserved, without a wealth of artifice, kitsch and nostalgia.

The visitor seeks in vain for stone cladding facades, slapped over reinforced concrete, nor does he/or she find a trace of those pedestrian precincts lined with shops for tourists suffering from their daily dose of TV soap operas, whose elegant and eye-catching window displays are decorated with knickknacks and Provençal fabrics made in China. There is no trace of self-proclaimed artists' studios or the second homes of unscrupulous investors who are eager to put their money into property values.

Only a stone's throw from Greater Avignon – which will soon be linking up with Greater Nîmes – from the Montpellier-Paris TGV train route and the A9, the visitor can explore unexpected landscapes that have remained curiously intact, rolling hills of unexpected beauty, a wild, rocky landscape with the look of virgin territory that is utterly magnificent, despite the 2000 years or so of viticulture. The visitor will also discover a society that appears to be very divided, clannish, lacking consistency, jealous of its privileges, habits and customs, yet one that throughout its history has been able to continually renew itself and band together when faced with threats, a solidarity that gives it the ability to fight, to distance itself and to overcome any danger of implosion or explosion. It is not an ideal, exemplary society in which everyone or almost everyone is someone's cousin, a community of interests consisting of individuals who, taken separately from each other, retain the habit of grumbling and are always doubting village solidarity, neighbourliness, complaining about their elected representatives, people who are richer or less poor and past achievements. Yet as soon as they come together, they form the links of an unbreakable chain of solidarity, that is refractory against anything which the outside world attempts to impose on them by force. This is a community that is jealous of the assertion that the grape-grower remains in a privileged minority but it is aware that it is this grape-grower and wine-maker who brings it wealth, consisting of old men without nostalgia and young men without blinkers, many of whom have left for foreign parts so they can return all the better for it and live close to the development of their living space. The community is happy to welcome the stranger as the purveyor of new blood, it integrates him and very soon converts into a confirmed Tavel native, through marriage, but anyone who deliberately sets himself apart remains so forever, without any means of recourse.

It is there that I found a wine that appears to be of ancient lineage, crumbling under the weight of uncertain traditions, overtaken by the fashion for fruity rosés, benefiting from technology, clarets at the peak of their glory, champagnes that are vinous, modern red wines and white wines from the Rhône region that are precise and generous, state-of-the-art Italian wines, Spanish and Portuguese wines with an unbeatable quality-for-pleasure ratio, but which, in truth, are more lively than ever. Of the fifty or so cuvées bottled in Tavel by thirty five independent bottlers and the cooperative cellar, I never tasted a poorly produced wine. What I found was a range of thirty, even forty, very different styles each of which represents – miraculously – a share of the true Tavel.

So it isn't me who created this work and introduced the imagery, but rather the people of Tavel, the men and women who themselves have created the wines. In the course of these pages, they will be telling their stories with pride, humility, love, respect and passion.

Let's get one thing straight. This book is not an advertising puff. It was only dictated to me by events, by the result of my research and my encounters, as well as by my professional consciousness. Tavel will not be transformed into a literary artifice in order to illustrate a perfect world, one that is perfectly illusory. Nor is it a laboratory experiment nor a socio-cultural computer simulation created for research purposes. Tavel remains an original microcosm in which human nature breathes, conspires and transpires. There is nothing in Tavel that is better than elsewhere. After having seen Tavel and drunk Tavel, you will not see the world in a new light. It will just seem not quite so bad.

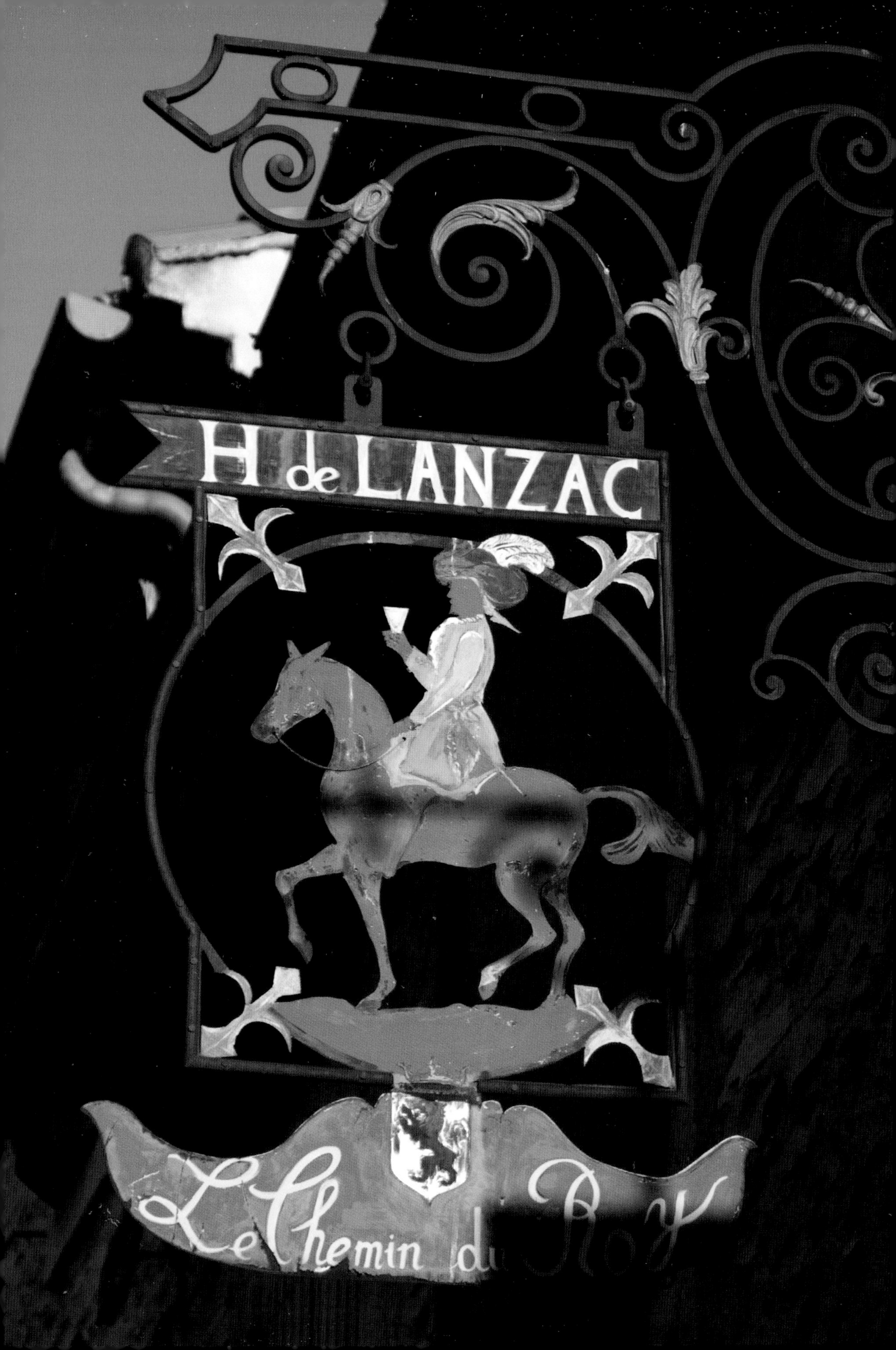
H de LANZAC
Le Chemin

INTRODUCTION

After many years without returning to Tavel, I went back in 2010 in order to write an article for the trade press. I did so almost reluctantly, my mind cluttered with mitigating feelings. Not because I'm a snob about rosés like so many of my colleagues, quite the opposite. Having been raised on the great wines of Bordeaux, Burgundy, Piedmont and Champagne, I have a predilection for all the fine, elegant, sincere and refreshing wines. Despite the job I have been doing for the past twenty-five years, I consider myself a drinker, above all, too often constrained to exercise my talents of a taster to meet the requirements of my occupation.

From my point of view, the Tavel rosé, supported by the advertising slogans of a bygone age, such as: 'Tavel, capital of rosé' or 'Tavel, France's premier rosé', appeared to me to be too heavy, alcoholic and oxidative. I imagined all the wine-makers of Tavel, joined in a cooperative, peasants and polluters who had been overtaken by events, heirs fattened on the manna that fell to a previous generation.

Of course, I was completely wrong. For the past decade, the inhabitants of Tavel, strengthened by their cooperative and the increasing number of vineyards at the forefront of progress, have had the ability to challenge themselves and make their domains more fresher, more exciting and fruitier, thanks to the vineyards that are now better and better tended producing healthier more natural wines. They have also learned to promote them and explain them better. That is because Tavel is a complex wine, one that is not easy to understand – and that may be its only fault. It suffers, above all, from a misunderstanding, that of being associated with rosé wines.

Tavel is not, in fact, a rosé. Tavel is a pale red wine, the 'colour of rubies tinted with gold' or even 'the colour of pale rubies tinted with topaz', two of the historic descriptions of Tavel that ought to be been inscribed in the definition of the AOC Tavel. Except that, officially, this type of wine does not exist. Œnology in its present state is capable of distinguishing only between red, white and rosé wines, naturally sweet wines, dessert wines, sparkling wines and so on, but not 'gold-tinted ruby wines' nor 'light red wines, high in alcohol content, made from grapes harvested from three complementary types of low-yielding terroir, macerated for a night or two at low temperature, then bottled, most of the time, without ageing in wood, suitable for being drunk young but which often improve with age'.

So such a wine is called a 'rosé de Tavel', although it ought to be simply called 'Tavel' and be entered in the world heritage of humanity. Creating a whole, separate category of wines for a production area that may well be historic and of quality but which is absolutely tiny, would only be pretentious. Currently, at the most extensive of its boundaries, the Tavel appellation barely covers 1,000 hectares of vineyards and produces an average of five million bottles a year. No other outcomes are possible –Tavel is one of the rosés, it is even historically, by reputation and quality, the greatest rosé in France.

It sells well and at a high price, thanks to its special status, its quality and its rarity, and thanks to the talent of the wine-makers of Tavel who have enhanced its reputation. But it is selling to an ageing population, consisting mainly of the French. It has been slow to make itself known and be acknowledged on the coveted export market. Faced with this David of the French wine trade, armed with his sling in the form of a bottle stamped 'rosé' which is not actually a rosé, Tavel can only stand by and witness the striking power of a rosé, a Bordeaux claret and the pink panthers of Provence and Languedoc, all of which are just as historic, but which are wines made from harvests over a vast territory, four times the size of Tavel, often more fertile, less exposed to strong winds and the burning sun, more productive. These vineyards of long tradition can also be easily mechanised. So Tavel's future is by no means a bed of roses.

This having been established, must one be resigned to producing red wine and white wine in Tavel, in the same way as in Lirac, the neighbouring village, which makes an historic Côtes-du-Rhône, but which has soil and exposures comparable to those of Tavel, and where numerous inhabitants of Tavel own vines? The terroir would permit this.

In fact the lower part of Tavel, consisting of well-drained sandy soil mixed with pebbles and a little clay, which is considered the historic part of the vineyard, is the favoured terroir for the finest rosé, with its lively bouquet. But the part of the vineyard that stretches over the terraces of smooth pebbles that stretches from Châteauneuf-du-Pape on the left bank of the Rhône to Costières de Nîmes on the right bank would be just as suitable for red wines that would have little need to envy Châteauneuf-du-Pape. As for the most recent area of the vineyard, situated on white limestone *lauses*, might also produce quality white wines, thanks to the state-of-the-art technologies used to make Tavel, such as cold settling and accurate control of the fermentation temperatures.

Yet despite the irreproachable quality of Lirac's wines, the name of Lirac is familiar to no one or hardly anyone. Red, rosé or white Liracs are harder to sell and a great deal cheaper than Tavel. Consequently, there is no better way for a wine-maker in Lirac, or even a maker of Côtes-du-Rhône, to advance himself than to acquire a plot or two in Tavel, however small it might be. Giving up the *monocru*, grapes grown in a single vineyard, would not seem to be a suitable solution.

The way that the people of Tavel are dealing with the current crisis seems to be the right one. Faced with the vagaries of globalisation and increasing competition, they are diversifying the styles, navigating with the assurance of a tightrope-walker between tradition and modernity, superficially enhancing their wine with a few borrowings from afar and references to current fashions. There is no need to make a radical change for the wine to be appreciated, these small retouches are sufficient to enable it to be better known.

The creed of the people of Tavel, that of a healthy wine produced from a protected environment, is part of this approach. The production of Tavel is sliding progressively from a reasoned culture – something that no longer actually means anything – to biological culture that is gaining more and more supporters. In the medium term, this could even be inscribed in the appellation decree because it has become an irrefutable sales pitch.

Tavel is the most contemporary wine there is, a very model for wine in the third millennium, just like champagne or fino sherry to which I would compare it. It is perfectly suited for adaptation to changing consumption habits. It can be drunk at any time, in any season and with any dish. Combining all these advantages, it can replace white wine, red wine and rosé, and even champagne or sweet dessert wines. It is as dainty and fresh as the finest Provence rosés, mineral and suave as a Puligny-Montrachet, elegant as a champagne from the Côte des Blancs, heady as a Gevrey-

Chambertin. It can be drunk by the glass as a daily habit or consumed by the bottle on more auspicious occasions.

In order to do this, it is sufficient to learn it, understand it and become intoxicated by its fragrances of flowers, spices, the *garrigue*, yellow fruits and berries. Its dense texture in which alcohol does not mean heaviness, but rather vinosity and sugar content, thanks to its structure, freshness and thus its general balance needs to be appreciated. It can be matched without prejudice with any type of food, from pizza to stew, from a selection of raw vegetables to a spicy dish, from classic French cooking to the cuisines of the world. It can be drunk in any atmosphere, whether beside the swimming-pool or at the fireside and it goes just as well with reading a good book to accompanying and finely spiced cigar from Dominica or a strong, mature Havana.

LEARNING AND UNDERSTANDING

At a universal exposition about twenty years ago, while trying to identify and thus better understand their little country, a few Swiss intellectuals stated: 'Switzerland does not exist'. Naturally this triggered an outcry and they were threatened with excommunication, banishment, and even crucifixion in the public square.

At the risk of exposing myself to the same danger, I dare to use the same provocation: Tavel does not exist. At the very most, one might speak of Tavels in the plural, since each wine-maker interprets the wine in his own way, just as a jazz musician who closely accompanies the rhythmic, harmonic and melodic design of a number that is very accurately described as a 'standard', so as to have the freedom to distance himself from the melody and thus improvise his own refrain. No one is more liberated than the person who happily accepts the rules created by his own conscience.

But beware! Nothing is due to chance, neither in the playing of a jazz musician, however 'free' it might appear, nor in the labours of a Tavel wine-maker. Everything has been thought through, developed, inspired, mastered. The improvisation of which I speak is something referred to in the English-speaking world as 'instant composing' and not the superficial talent for cobbling something together of which the alleged rigid and stolid Northerners accuse the allegedly dishonest and amoral pilferers of the South!

Tavel's wine-makers – male and female – never allow themselves to be guided by chance. Every year, depending on the data of that vintage, they carefully compose the Tavel cuvée or cuvées, embellishing or impregnating the basic partition with their own style.

The basis for Tavel is dictated to them by the three types of terroir, each providing a style of grape must that is very different, due to the vine stocks used, such as Grenache, kings of the southern vine stocks, supplemented by around ten others, including Mourvèdre, Cinsault and white or pink Clairette. Finally, there is control over yield which must barely exceed thirty hectolitres per hectare. Thanks to carefully chosen and adapted techniques (to be studied in detail in the third part of this book), the result is an archetypal wine of a fairly dark pink colour that is smooth due to its richness in natural alcohol, fairly dense and always well structured, a suave, long-lasting finale in the mouth supported by this structure and richness. Tavel is a maceration rosé or, more accurately, a red wine that is light in flavour and colour but at the same time one that has definite power because it is warm and well structured. For the past few years, it has noticeably been more aromatic and with constantly improving production.

From this point on, the Tavel paths diverge. On the one hand, there are those who would move closer to the modern rosé with its paler hue, a lower alcohol content and a minerality that is highly sought after. On the other hand, there are those who would bring it closer to a red wine due to its transparent ruby colour and the powerful tannins that are admired by some and condemned by others. There are even Tavel wines of such finesse that one might be tempted to confuse them with white wines of character. There are also those whose fashionable candy-pink colouring only superficially hide the true Tavel. And finally, there are all the variations and nuances in between.

The differences are sometimes subtle, however, like the variations played by a jazzman from one jam session to the next. To learn how to recognise them, it is not enough to taste them with the lips and spit them out again, they need to be drunk again and again, slowly, patiently, with moderation and self-control. That is because Tavel, at its highest degree, also teaches us to do so, to exercise restraint in order to be able to taste for as long as possible the pleasure it gives us instead of pouncing on a canapé after two hastily swallowed glasses.

The choice of the right glass and a suitable temperature are both crucial. Despite recent efforts to precisely determine the date of the harvest, transport and chilling of the grapes to retain a maximum of precursors of the aromas, Tavel is nevertheless not exactly an aromatic wine. Of course, specially selected yeasts could be used in order to enhance, or even grant it more bouquet, but could it then be described as a wine of the terroir? Better to accept things as they are and take them into account. A tulip glass that is relatively, of the type used to sample white Burgundy, claret or Chianti suits it perfectly.

Depending on the type, it should be served in the glass at eight degrees for the lighter wines and at ten or even twelve degrees centigrade for the stronger wines, and it can then warm, depending on the ambient temperature to ten, twelve or even fourteen degrees, the ideal temperature to sniff out the delicate richness of the bouquet of a Tavel. Contrary to all other wines, Tavel seems to be scorched if served with ice! If this is done, it tastes of nothing, unless it is of alcohol.

An additional advantage of the tulip glass is the quite wide and slightly curved mouth that makes it possible to appreciate the smoothness of the wine as the mouth relaxes, whereas a small balloon glass with a narrow opening would give one the impression of alcohol that rather burns the tongue and pursed lips. To serve it at the right temperature, there is nothing simpler and more practical than using a wine cellar or a cabinet to bring it up to the correct temperature. A good refrigerator or a freezer with a few wine cooling jackets of the 'Rapid Ice' or similar types, plus a suitable thermometer will do just as well, however.

If you are caught unawares, don't be afraid to put a whole bottle in a freezer or the freezing compartment of the refrigerator for thirty minutes or so, and ignore the outraged protests of the purists. In a little blind tasting, wearing a blindfold, I was easily able to distinguish between an INAO[1] glass and a claret glass filled with the same Tavel that had been placed

under my nose. But I was absolutely incapable of distinguishing between Tavel taken from the freezer and a Tavel cooled in my wine cabinet, despite the fact that they were at almost the same degree of temperature. Twenty or thirty minutes in the freezer (the only thing is not to forget it's there!) than three weeks in a refrigerator that smells of leeks and catfood! I apologise for being so categorical, but public enemy number one of any wine that needs to be served chilled is not the freezer but a refrigerator that contains food! You can keep an opened bottle of Tavel for four or five days in cool place – even if, in my house, an uncorked bottle of Tavel is a bottle to be eliminated – but keep it away from smells!

If you have the wherewithal and faithful friends who like paying homage to your cellar, do not fail to ask for a magnum of Tavel. Not only is this a handsome and generous gesture, but the

Tavel that comes out of the bottle seems to be better, rounder, which a stronger bouquet and more finesse. And if you wish to do so, it keeps even better.

That is because Tavel can indeed be aged, although this is not an absolute necessity. I honestly believe that most contemporary Tavel wines are at the top of their form and expression between eight and eighteen months after harvesting. If you happen to forget that you have a bottle of Tavel made in a good year in your cellar, don't worry, you are in for a nice surprise. After four, six, or ten and even twenty years, Tavel has something very special about it, something of the *rancio*², with notes of cocoa, walnuts, leather, wild mushrooms, white truffles, and sometimes even quinces, and it is then reminiscent of an old Tawny port or a very old Mercurey. You should then serve it in a carafe, which will also benefit

Tavel that contains a small hint of reduction, even if this 'defect', which only recently was very typical of Tavel – and of most champagnes! – is tending to disappear. By choosing an elegant, tall, clear glass carafe that will show its sparkling colour to its best advantage, you will understand why this type of wine was once preferred by the crowned heads of Europe about which more will be said in the following chapter.

1- The wineglass shape recommended by the Institut national des appellations d'origine, the French organisation responsible for

2- Rancio = a wine that has been fortified in the same way as madeira. Rancio wines are found in south-western France.

HISTORY

To live in the present and project oneself into the future, one needs to study the past and do so with humility, accepting that the history of grape-growing and wine-making, so often usurped and converted into a selling point, does not excuse defects and is no guarantee of quality. So many ancient vineyards have disappeared and many will disappear in the future, but their history does not exclude and could, at the very most, explain why this is so. Other vineyards will be born and will record their annals in order to enrich our grape-growing and wine-making culture. Wine does not need a long tradition in order to exist, but it needs to be told in order to be understood, transmitted and respected.

If God emanates from the discussions between man and his conscience, He will disappear when the last believer has gone. If terroir is the result of a meeting between man and nature, it cannot exist without him. A soil may prove to be se fertile or sterile, arid or rich, but it is not a terroir. For it become one, other factors need to be present – the soil and the sub-soil, the climate, the seasons and their variations, the sun and the clouds, the microclimate consisting of light, shade and rain. In addition, there is the specific culture attached to a place, to its relationship with the communication routes than enable the transport or the distribution of the product of the harvest.

The creation of a great wine is the result of a fortunate and productive pact between man and his terroir. The human being cultivates the land, enhances it, gives it its significance, transmits it but he cannot invent it. At the very most, he can do his best to discover it, in the true sense of the word dis-cover, meaning to remove its wild covering of undergrowth, stones, grass and woodland.

The importance of grape-growing terroir is much older than the history of grape-growing which leaves us neutral, often inadequate data, due to a lack of verifiable sources. It contains information that is useful for understanding and respect for the knowledge acquired by generations of grape-growers and wine-makers, at the cost of effort and privation. The history may contain useless, and even misleading, information that are in danger of distorting the truth and distracting the superficial glance of the observer. History can be manipulated and exploited, be rewritten and interpreted.

To start with, we shall simply attempt to incorporate the history of the wines of France with restraint and prudence, without being carried away, into the small amount of information available to us concerning the history of Tavel wine.

We should emphasise that the village of Tavel is in Lower Languedoc, despite the fact that the wine is currently classified as a Côtes-du-Rhône. The vine is certified to have been cultivated in Languedoc since the fifth century BC. It was developed first by the Greeks, then by the Romans and eventually extended right around the Mediterranean basin. The province of Narbonne, the *provincia narbonensis*, founded about one hundred years BC by the proconsul Domitius, was one of the most prosperous in the Roman Empire. The olive tree and the vine flourished here and provided the raw material for long-lasting trade between the North and the South. Wine, which offered the most reliable and thus the most enviable added value, was transported in amphoras that were mass-produced or in tanker ships. Diodorus of Sicily, a Greek historian living in Rome during the first century BC, commented on this commercial activity in the following terms: 'The natural avarice of many Italian merchants exploits the passion for wine possessed by the Gauls. On the ships that sail down navigable waterways or on chariots that ride over the plains, they transport their wine, from which they make incredible profits, to such an extent that they will barter a single amphora for a slave, so that the purchaser releases his servant to them to pay for his drink' (Roger Dion, *Histoire de la vigne et du vin en France*, Paris, 1959).

In order to ensure the long-lasting nature of their territorial conquests, the Romans assigned to their faithful legionnaires land that bordered their most

important communications axes, so that they would build their villas there and cultivate the surrounding land. The right to plant vines and olive trees was thus granted only to true Romans but in order to increase their profits, these Romans often transferred part of their holding to the natives who would maintain some of the vineyards on their behalf. The towns and villages of today were often created from these Roman villas or Roman agriculture.

In 92 AD, the Emperor Domitian found himself forced to ban any new vine plantings in Italy and ordered that half of those in the Roman provinces be destroyed. 'At the time, Rome was acting no differently than Brussels did in 1980', as Jean Clavel reminds us in his book, *Le 21ᵉ siècle des vins du Languedoc*, published by Editions Causse in 1999.

Just like his successors from the Middle Ages until today, Domitian's aim was not to abolish grape-growing but to restrict it. He was simply attempting to secure his prosperity, guaranteeing that fertile land would be used for growing grain and thus feeding a growing population, thus avoiding abandoning the land to mass grape-growing that was liable to produce wines of poor quality. Yet despite this edict, and tall those that followed it at important times in the history of grape cultivation, the vine continued to expand.

The current Tavel appellation – the name derives from the Latin *villa tavellis,* that is first mentioned in the thirteenth century, and which became *Tavels,* then Tavel – was ideally suited because it was located on an important communication route between the *oppidum* of Roquemaure and Nîmes. When ploughing, numerous Tavel

grape-growers have discovered remains that are probably linked to this trade, such as fragments of amphoras, broken tiles and pottery shards, vases decorated with bunches of grapes. And in the Bouvette district, the remains have been uncovered of what appear to be Gallo-Roman baths dating from between the first and the third century AD (Jacques Reboul, *Essai sur l'histoire du vin de Tavel*). Although there is not one iota of proof for this theory, Tavel might have grown its first vines on land that was not suitable for food crops.

Between the fall of the Roman Empire and the end of the Middle Ages, few documents show evidence of sustainable and high-quality viticulture in Lower Languedoc, and consequently in Tavel itself. The transport of foodstuffs, including wine, moved from the Mediterranean which had become unsafe, to the Atlantic, enabling England and the Low Countries to prosper. The port of Bordeaux and its local wines also benefited, and Paris was supplied by wines from grapes grown in the vicinity, as well as from Burgundy and Champagne. Starting in the tenth century, these provinces found themselves in the promised land of wine-making. It was not until the early eighteenth century that agriculture was fully revived again in the French Midi (Jacques Reboul).

In the days when the popes resided in Avignon, the pontifical court accounted for a considerable amount of the wine produced near the city and possible also in Tavel. In 1358, the year in which Pope Innocent VI was forced to sell his own silver and jewellery in order to replenish the coffers of a city which had been ravaged by plague and famine, the archives of the Popes' Palace nevertheless mention a transaction by a wine steward concerning a certain quantity of wine traded with the priory of Montézargues, which even today remains the finest centre of Tavel wine-making (Jacques Reboul). After the Popes had returned to Rome, they continued their link with the wines of the Comtat Venaissin which remained in their possession from 1274 – when Philippe II of Burgundy, known as Philip the Bold, sold it to Pope Gregory X – until the French Revolution. Thus three-quarters of the wines served at table in the Holy See came from the vineyards of the lower Rhone Valley, between Châteauneuf (which became known as Châteauneuf-du-Pape in the nineteenth century), on the left bank, and half a dozen villages situated on the right bank between the two river ports of Beaucaire and Pont Saint-Esprit. The two villages of Chusclan and Laudun are mentioned. Several hundred years later they would constitute, along with Tavel, the first AOC in the world, which was named Côtes-du-Rhône, of which more later. Prior to the eighteenth century, Italy was almost the sole export outlet for the wines of the lower Rhone Valley.

By the late Middle Ages, the port city of Bordeaux, surrounded by rows of grape vines, constituted the stronghold of wine. It was ideally situated on the banks of the Garonne, and was filled with ships that could sail to the Gironde estuary, and thence to the Atlantic Ocean. When Eleanor of Aquitaine married the Plantagenet King of England Henry II, it fell to the English who ruled it for more than three hundred years. The city was proud of its commercial 'privilege' that dated from the fourteenth century and had made it famous. This enabled the merchants of the city to sell their wine first and they exported it in quantities that were phenomenal for the era. They were able to trade Bordeaux wines before those of the High Country were allowed to enter the city, except in bad years when they permitted the 'perking up'

of Bordeaux wines of doubtful quality. Grapes harvested from the marl slopes that extended to the outskirts of the city were then of a 'clairet' or 'claret' colour, the name the English still use to designate the red wines of Bordeaux. The privilege was abolished in 1776, some time after the city was recaptured by the kings of France.

The wines of Bordeaux were a rather pallid ruby colour like all fine red wines for centuries. It was not until the seventeenth century that they grew slightly darker. They had been forced to change with the times due to competition from the new drinks exported from the colonies and wines whose grapes had ripened in the southern sun, which threatened to replace this universal drink that had created the wealth of the middle classes and the nobility. Coffee was stronger and darker in colour than fine French wine. The first coffee-houses opened in Paris in the 1670s, and then came chocolate, along with the powerful, blood-coloured wines of Spain which entered France following the Franco-Spanish wars of 1635, the Treaty of the Pyrenees in1659 and Louis XIV's marriage to the Spanish infanta.

South of Bordeaux, on his family estate, after his elders cleared a stony outcrop and built a handsome mansion on it which was soon to be known as a wine-making château, Arnaud III of Pontac, a merchant and president of the city parliament, hugely increased his income from the proceeds of grape-growing and wine-making, by improving the production methods. In 1666, he sent his son to London to open a restaurant called *Pontac's Head* which stayed open until 1780 (see Marcel Lachiver). Despite the ravages of the Great Fire of London in 1666, the English capital was in the process of unseating Paris as the cultural capital of Europe. *Chez Pontac* soon became the favourite watering-hole of dandies, poets and philosophers, offering delicious French food and wine made on the family estate at Haut-Brion. Three years earlier, on 10 April 1663, Samuel Pepys, Secretary to the Admiralty, had noted in his famous diary: '*And here (I) drank a sort of French wine, called Ho Bryan, that hath a good and most particular taste that I never met with*'. The wine-loving secretary is thus referring to a very special flavour and one can detect a certain measure of surprise and rather than an unlimited enthusiasm. This new style of wine, more deeply coloured, more tannic, more vinous and denser, that had little in common with the sprightly, light wines that had been drunk hitherto, took some getting used to.

Contrary to the coarse, vin ordinaire, known as *vinum rubrum* with its bright red colour, often enhanced with the addition of elderberries and other artifices, the fine wine of the Middle Ages and the Renaissance, known as *vinum clarum,* or claret, was paler in colour and drunk in its pure state. It was easily digested and elegant, being insufficient vinous for dilution with water. It was

thus a luxury item that only a wealthy aristocrat could afford. The wine of Champagne, from the slopes of Ay, Hautvillers or Avenay, made from red grapes, became the basis for this drink of the fortunate elite. It was pale ruby in colour, fine, delicate and with a pleasant raspberry flavour. As an example, there is the story of a Parisian bourgeois who offered a *clairet* wine to a friend in 1550. The friend so enjoyed it that he exclaimed: 'I drunk it down in one go, I was so thirsty (…) Oh such liquor, such raspberry!' (Roger Dion). Three centuries earlier, the Duke of Guines proudly served a thirsty Bishop of Reims who had asked him for a drink, a glass of wine that was as clear as water, thus illustrating that the wines of Lower Burgundy had nothing to fear from the wines of Champagne. At the time, a rather insipid colour was not considered to be a defect, quite the contrary, it was believed to be the ultimate proof of the quality of a wine, guaranteeing its purity, cleanliness, finesse and digestibility.

The 'new French claret', also drunk without the addition of water, was a luxury drink produced from a château estate and thus provided with indisputable letters of nobility – at least as far as a French nouveau riche bourgeois or a London dandy were concerned – must have surprised, and even astonished, many. Its success was nevertheless assured, the 'new French claret' conquered the world. From then on, the colour and style of a great Bordeaux wine, which was already ten to twenty times dearer after its creation than ordinary claret, became the unique and absolute point of reference for every great red wine. That is, except for Tavel wine, the only survivor of a wine-making culture that declared: 'If I cannot see through it, the wine has something to hide from me'. But let's not be premature, we shall be discussing the very particular colour and style of Tavel wine further on.

Starting in the mid-seventeenth century, wine-drinking habits changed. The standard of living improved; even in the countryside, the lower middle classes and peasantry were able to afford better quality wines. The hard frost of 1709 destroyed much of the southern grapevines and they did not match their previous yield until two or three years later. This caused the wine-merchants of Paris and Lyon to seek their produce further south, in order to quench the population's thirst.

As demand increased, so did the price of wine. The French Midi witnessed a absolute rush to plant vines which was immediately criticised by the aristocracy who looked unfavourable upon the competition it faced from small land-owners who had begun to clear the land and cultivate the vine. The result was a deterioration in the quality of badly run vineyards, grapes harvested too early, yields that were too high and quality wines being diluted with inferior ones. The ruling class retorted by imposing restrictions, and even a ban on planting which was immediately denounced by the victims of these restrictions. One of them was the philosopher Montesquieu who had to suspend the planting of his vineyard at La Brède near Bordeaux and expressed his displeasure in a memorandum in which he comments: 'The Guyenne (…) must supply the foreigner with different sorts of wines, dependent upon the diversity of its terroirs. The tastes of foreigners are changing all the time, to such an extent that there is not a single type of wine that was fashionable twenty years ago that remains so today; to such an extent that wines that were rejected at the time are now held in high esteem. This inconsistent taste has to be followed, and [vines] planted or grubbed up accordingly'.

In 1725, despite such protests, the ban on planting order for the Guyenne was extended to the whole kingdom. Only six years later, it was once again abolished, on the condition however that it could be proved that the land to be planted was not suitable for any other crop.

The year 1681 saw the opening of the canal du Midi which created a link between Sète and Bordeaux. In 1748, two Dutch merchants complained that the city of Bordeaux had seized their cargo of 310 bottles of Côtes-du-Rhône wines (Roger Dion). In 1776 the privilege granted to the wines of Bordeaux was abolished and the wine-making areas of Languedoc and the lower Rhone valley once more gained free access to the world markets.

Demand was strong and there was plenty of competition, however, from Bordeaux, Anjou, Burgundy and la Champagne had the wind in their sails, and Spain and Portugal also threw themselves into the fray. A plethora of wines destined for the Low Countries or England passed through the two major sea ports of Jerez and Porto. The abuses continued and it became vital to protect the production of quality wines.

In 1703, the Treaty of Methuen was ratified. This treaty governed commerce between England and Portugal. The English, who had hitherto greatly enjoyed the exceptional wines of France, suddenly transformed into port-drinkers, while on the other hand the Portuguese granted favourable treatment to British cotton and woollen cloth.

The Douro, Portugal's major wine-producing region, was in ferment. The traditional trade that was faithful to its values was supplanted by unscrupulous pedlars of dreams who cared for neither the quality nor the origin of what they sold. Production increased, but still remained inadequate and was unable to satisfy demand. The fraud caused the downfall. The customers complained, exports vacillated, and prices went into freefall.

In 1756, thanks to the initiative of the Marquis de Pombal, The General Company of Agriculture of the Vines of the Upper Douro was created. The producing region was delineated by 335 boundary markers around the area that produced fine wines, the only ones suitable for export to England. So it was Portugal, and not France, that actually invented the AOC, the Appellation d'Origine Contrôlée, the controlled designation of origin. But was Portugal really the first?

The Tavel town hall contains a real treasure, namely the record books of the deliberations of the consuls of Tavel, a sort of town council, traced by the hands of 'those who knew how to write' at the time.

The document recording the deliberations of 8 April 1716 (see the photo on page 24), reads as follows:

'… Before me and in the house of Sr Pierre Odoyer, there presented themselves Mathieu Roudil and Claude Vissac, modern consuls of the place known as Tavel. As was also proposed by these consuls that the community of the place having no other means of being able to support payment of the royal charges and monies and other taxation which the sale of their wine which is highly reputed and which is effectively sought after and provides almost all of the income for this community which nevertheless through considerable abuse – there have entered into the place of the harvests and wine strangers who have entirely destroyed the reputation and good quality of the wine from the true vintage of the place which has a fine reputation which it is necessary to maintain and prevent any other grape harvest or wine entering this place without which the true wine of Tavel would entirely lose its reputation and the inhabitants in this place would be reduced to utter poverty and incapable of making the payment of the royal monies and other taxation… this having been heard by Mr Vincent Odoyer, Sr Pierre Odoyer, Jean Jaume, Antoine Avril, Jean Charasse, Pol Guilhard, Jean Chambon, André Odoyer, Pierre Roche, all of them inhabitants of the said place. Signed Charasse, Jaume. Those who know how to write: Pallejay, clerk to the council'.

Translated into modern French, the basic formula for the deliberations of 1716 demands protection for the origins of the wines made from the harvest in the territory of Tavel. This demand was repeated and supplemented several times during the last decades that followed, with even greater insistence. For example, we can learn even more from the deliberations of 14 January 1731. They note that, for the last few years, the inhabitants have planted most of their arid and sterile land with vines and yet for the past thirty or so years, the population has greatly increased. According to contemporary writings, Tavel wine was of 'exquisite goodness',

'it travels well and is sent as far as Paris, Rome and throughout the province and the merchants are willing to pay more for it than for all the other wines of Languedoc'. Consequently, there was a proposal to imitate the villages of Lirac and Roquemaure where 'the entry of foreign wine is forbidden on pain of confiscation of the said wine and payment of a considerable fine …'.

As a result of these deliberations, emissaries from Roquemaure accompanied by two resident of Tavel (or vice-versa, depending on point of view) travelled to Montpellier to visit the king's intendant in order to petition for the right to protect the origin of their wine.

History teaches us that their petition was granted. In 1737 – this being several years before the restriction imposed in the Upper Douro – the wines of a bare dozen villages on the right bank of the southern reaches of the Rhône, including Tavel, Chusclan, Laudun, Roquemaure and Lirac, obtained the right to mark their barrels with the letters C.d.R. (Côte-du-Rhône) and the vintage of the harvest, and were thus henceforward protected by the earliest AOC *(appellation d'origine contrôlée)* in the world.

Despite what the great scholar Roger Dion has written – he is fully pardoned for his very minor error – it was indeed *Côte du Rhône* in the singular and thus only one bank that was mentioned, rather than *Côtes-du-Rhône* in the plural. The royal order, by endorsing the deliberations of the General Council of Roquemaure on 6 August 1693 and 10 September 1737, also teaches us that Roquemaure indeed took the initiative for this protection, and that at least part of the wording used in the Tavel deliberations was borrowed from the Roquemaure deliberations. This is not surprising since Roquemaure served as the port of embarkation for the surrounding villages. Here is an extract from the order (see Jacques Maby, *La trame du vignoble*, page 107):

'The order in council of 23 January 1657 (sic) shall be executed in its form and content. There is once again a prohibition on all to introduce, into the town and its outskirts and its land, any foreign

wine and any [grape] harvest for making wine in the town and its territory, on pain of confiscation of the wine, the barrels and the harvest as well as the wagon and the beasts of burden drawing it, and a fine of 100 pounds.

'No inhabitant, merchant or anyone else shall be permitted to store in a cellar or storehouse in Roquemaure any foreign wine brought to the port of the Rhône, on any pretext. To obviate any abuse that may be committed by passing off wines of poor vintages for those of genuinely good vintages, such as Roquemaure and the neighbouring and contiguous places and parishes with those of Tavel, Lirac, Saint-Laurent-des-Arbres, Saint-Geniès-de-Comolas, Orsan, Chusclan, Codoret and others that are of superior quality, they shall be marked (…) being full and not otherwise, with a brand containing the three letters C.d.R. signifying Côte du Rhône (…)'.

In the book written by the French historian and specialist in French country life, Marcel Lachiver, *Vins, vignes et vignerons* (quoted frequently in this book), there is a reference to the history of wine-making and although he devotes whole pages to the birth of the great wines of Bordeaux, this revolutionary idea is worth only a few lines: '… (It was) the era in which Tavel made an arrangement with several parishes in the vicariate of Uzès to place restrictions on wines purporting to originate from the Côte du Rhône (…) A *cru* and a vintage, these are indeed the beginnings of a grand wine'.

So here we are, with proof to support the claim. The reputation of the wine of Tavel as being exceptional dates back to the early eighteenth century. It was sold at a higher price than the other wines of Languedoc. Yet the only source that affirms its higher quality originates from the archives of the Tavel town hall. If we do not want to be accused of partiality we shall also need an independent source. Fortunately, such a source exists. We owe it to the wine merchant and writer André Jullien, whose book entitled *Topographie de tous les vignobles connus*, published in 1816, then re-edited and corrected in 1832, is the first work of reference listing all of the known vineyards

in France and throughout the world, describing them and classifying them into several types and categories.

Jullien distinguishes between the various types: dry wine, dessert wine and liqueur wine de liqueur; by their colour: red and white (but no rosé yet); by the three principal grades: fine wines, *vin ordinaire* and common wines. He then ranks them in five categories, from first class to fifth class.

The fine wines are divided into two other types based on their general balance and their characteristic vigour and bouquet. These wines have the advantage of acquiring many additional qualities as they age. Common wines are not kept for long enough to acquire the necessary balance. Their main defect is thus to be coarse or poor and sickly. They often have an unpleasant flavour of

the terroir. Their body consists of coarse matter that disappears in a few months. They may appear to be delicate, but this delicacy is due solely to the absence of colour, body and spirits (alcohol content). *Vins ordinaires* should be classified between fine wine and common wines.

The first class is reserved for fine wines of superior quality that are only harvested in a small number of *crus*; the second class is for fine wines of the first quality that are slightly more abundant; the third class contains fine and semi-fine wines, the fourth class *vins ordinaires* of first quality and the fifth class the other *vins ordinaires* as well as the common wines.

Thus, André Jullien, thanks to his precision, independence and lack of servility, taking little account of local susceptibilities in his descriptions of wines, has handed down reliable information

of major importance. So what does he write about Tavel? He writes that Tavel is one of the vineyards of the department of Gard, and thus still in Lower Languedoc. This département has about 75,000 hectares of vineyards, distributed in 355 communes, which produce red wine almost exclusively. Twenty per cent of the wines harvested are drunk locally, twenty per cent turned into brandy and the rest exported to the rest of France and abroad. Thirty-one types of grapes are grown, ten of them black, including Alicante (Grenache), Espar (Mourvèdre), Piquepoule (Picpoul) and Colitor (Calitor), seven red and eleven white, including Clairette. Grape-growing is the main farming activity in the département which provides the best wines in the province, whether fine wines for the table, or more ordinary wines to 'give quality' to wines that lack it. Tavel and Lirac

are classified as fine red wines of the first class. This is the text that follows the introduction, translated in its entirety:

'Wines of the first class: all of the vineyards in this first class are situated around Uzès.

CHUSCLAN, 11 kil. from Pont-Saint-Esprit, on the slope known as Tavel, produces pale-coloured wines that are fine, light, spirituous and agreeable; even though they are precocious, they can be kept for a long time. TAVEL, 5 kil. from Roquemaure, produces wines that are a little firmer and not as light as the previous ones, but very fine and very spirituous: they benefit from ageing. LIRAC, 24 kil. from Beaucaire and 32 kil. from Nîmes. The wines from this vineyard are from the same type as Tavel, and only differ from it by having a little more firmness and colour. SAINT-GENIES, 20 kil. from Pont-Saint-Esprit, produces wines that

share the qualities of those of Chusclan; except that they are darker in colour and less spirituous. LEDENON, 14 kil. from Nîmes, produces wines of the first cuvee that have a fine colour, and are strong and spirituous, with a very good flavour and a pleasant bouquet. SAINT-LAURENT-DES-ARBRES, 22 kil. from Pont-Saint-Esprit, produces wines of a deeper colour that are slightly less spirituous than those of Tavel; they are very good in warm years. The wines of the vineyards I have just mentioned, which are generally quite open in their flavour, are of equal quality to those of the third class of the Côte d'Or; they only differ in being more spirituous, which often gives them a mordant quality that makes them less pleasant; they also have less bouquet. All of them travel well on land and sea without deteriorating; in the trade they are normally lumped together under the name of fine

Languedoc wines'. (André Jullien, *Topographie de tous les vignobles connus*, third edition,1832).

Just for information – without going into it more in depth and certainly without a sub-text – it should be added that the wines of Roquemaure and Laudun, which are now classified as Côtes-du-Rhône, and those of Saint-Gilles, Bagnols and Jonquières, nowadays incorporated into Costières-de-Nîmes, produce 'only' second-class wines. Thus, Roquemaure, originator of the protection of the wines of the Côte du Rhône, appears by the early nineteenth century to have lost something of its superb quality of the previous century.

To complete this glimpse into the quality of the region's wines in that era, let us add two other villages which, a hundred years later, combined with Tavel, to create the first official *appellations d'origine* in the region. Like Tavel, Châteauneuf-du-Pape has been selected as being in the first class, producing 'based on ancient and new local and Spanish seedlings' delicate 'though warm' wines, that can be kept for three or four years. Cassis, near Marseille, produces 'the finest white wines in the province, sweet with a very pleasant taste, powerful and spirituous', costing three times more than the local red wine.

Note that André Jullien mentions the distance of each village from the closest port, such as Roquemaure, Beaucaire and Pont Saint-Esprit. The river thus remained the major means of transport. It was not until 1855, that the railway link between Montpellier and Paris was opened, and Tavel was never connected to it.

We can thus claim that in the early nineteenth century, based on a reputation stretching back a hundred years, the wine of Tavel was considered to be one of the greatest wines of France. It was one of the finest on the right bank of the lower Rhone Valley, which overall produced wines comparable to the great Burgundies of the third class, and thus to a Burgundy Villages such as a Beaune, a Vosne-Romanée, a Volnay or a Pommard in modern times.

Tavel already had a number of the same advantages that characterise it to this day. The colour is average, not as strong as that of the wines of Lirac and Saint-Laurent, but it is firm, full in the mouth, but very subtle and it improves with ageing, an absolute sign of quality at the time. Above all, it never followed the fashion of the tannic and acrid 'new French claret', nor of the 'big red that stains' which was the source of the wealth of the Béziers wine trade in the nineteenth century. Tavel wine remained close to the style of a great fine wine from an earlier age. Was this refusal to change, immutability or clairvoyance which has substituted the values of the past for the tastes of today? This will be examined later.

In 1819, when the French monarchy was restored and André Jullien's book was published, the Tavel vineyard covered 721 hectares and occupied two thirds of the cultivatable land of the village (see Jacques Maby). The wine was sold there at a high price thus producing a high profit. The French Revolution enabled the peasants to acquire a few more plots of vines. The manorial estates such as Aquéria, Manissy or even Trinquevedel, whose lord, Claude de Castellan, had been killed during the Revolution, were taken over by wealthy bourgeois. Just like the surrounding villages, for a hundred years, thanks to the solidarity of its inhabitants and their talent for defending their common interest, Tavel was able to resist oppression, fraud and competition. 'In 1860, Tavel produced nearly 15,000 hectolitres of wine, a yield close to 20 hectolitres per hectare', or so we are informed – again by Jacques Maby, who has closely studied the départemental and municipal archives. This is a more than respectable yield for the time, but far from the record yields of 200 hectolitres per hectare and more, produced in the plain of the Aude by the high-yielding hybrid stocks, that tolled the knell of the vineyards of Languedoc and from which the Côte-du-Rhône increasingly distanced itself.

The village made a profit of 250,000 francs. One hectare of vines yielded 300 francs a year, at a time when a blue-collar worker barely earned a third of that. At the time, the population of Tavel was 1,300, as against 600 in 1931 and 1,800 today.

The village built its public laundry, its church and its town hall, and many wine-merchants settled in the region, at Beaucaire, Roquemaure and Bagnols-sur-Cèze. The villagers of Tavel impatiently waited to be connected to the French rail network, which according to deliberations of the Tavel town hall on 3 August 1867: 'would give the commune a very great advantage, both by facilitating the transport of goods (…) and by dispensing with several bridges for which the taxes are very onerous as well as for the flow of our agricultural produce and especially our quite high-esteemed wines which would result in the arrival of a greater number of merchants (…)'. Their wine continues to be referred to as being of high quality, despite increasing competition from the vineyards of the left bank of the river which took advantage of the reputation of those on the right bank and the birth of Côtes-du-Rhône – in the plural – an appellation that was usurped according to the inhabitants of the right bank. And despite everything and everyone, Tavel retained its original colour.

The fashion continued, nevertheless, for darker and darker red wines. In his *Cours de l'agriculture pratique,* published in 1820, the agronomist Rougier de la Bergerie wrote:

'The most important point of emulation in the small vineyards planted with high-yielding stocks, is to obtain a lot of colour. (…) That is because from a sweet white wine, and unfortunately from other liquids, a wine is then created that is said to be a Burgundy; heads of households and owners of workshops also prefer highly coloured wines because they are suitable for the addition of water for reasons of economy. The opaque, dark colour is so sought after that the merchants in Limousin and Auvergne make buying trips to Limousin, Auvergne and Quercy, Périgord and Angoumois, but do not even bother to taste the wine; they merely fill a glass whose contents they then dash against a white wall; if the wall turns bright red, they buy it, and the price even depends on the intensity of the colour'.

In order to obtain the colour (without losing

yield!) that the market demanded and that was sought after, owners and dealers in Languedoc proceeded to make selections and create hybrids. In 1836, Louis Bouchet brought in the first harvest of a hybrid of Aramon and Teinturier stocks on his estate at Mauguio near Montpellier (see Marcel Lachiver). Simultaneously, as much from curiosity as for the purpose of continuing to experiment, American vine stocks, such as the black grape Isabelle with its strong raspberry flavour, was introduced in the Languedoc vineyards, as well as in Bordeaux.

In 1863, at Pujaut, only five kilometres from Tavel, a few vine plants died in a plantation whose travelling owner had probably wanted to embellish with a few American seedlings. No one paid much attention. Five years later, Jules-Emile Planchon of the Montpellier School of

Pharmacy, discovered a tiny insect on the dead stumps of a few plantings of Graveson vine in the département of Bouches-du-Rhône. He named the insect *phylloxera vastatrix*.

In 1880, two-thirds of vines growing in France had been attacked or destroyed by this pest imported from the New World. One of the most seriously affected departments was that of Gard, whose grapevine cultivation was reduced to 15,000 hectares, although ten years earlier it had covered nearly 90,000 hectares. The vineyards of Tavel suffered badly. In 1870, no more than 50 hectares of seedlings remained and they were sickly. It was not until 1977 that he village regained the area of 800 hectares of vines that had been recorded in 1868.

The Tavel solution was to switch other industries. Three silk–producing factories were set up, the

marble producers expanded their quarries to extract Tavel which even today has a high reputation. A few meagre deposits of phosphates were exploited. But in Tavel, there have been generations of wine-makers from father to son, and the switch barely got started. The result was an exodus –Tavel lost two-thirds of its population.

The fight against the crop pest began too timidly and too late. Although in Tavel reconstruction was swifter, of a higher quality, more thorough and long-lasting than in other comparable vineyards, even so it took fifty years, slowed down by two world wars and a major economic crisis. The reasons for the slowness are multiple and complex, too complex for them to be described in great detail here. Jacques Maby, who understands just how grape-growers and wine-makers think, as well as the microcosm of the village from which his family originates, provides one of the most convincing explanations in his veritable bible of the social geography of the Rhone vineyards:

'Phylloxera produced a serious psychological shock in a society dependent on wine. The total ruined that overwhelmed it also disabled it. Worse still, it destroyed any trust in the plant that had made its fortune and which was now so brutally abandoning it. Fight for the vine? It first needed to be loved! For its wine? For this, faith and respect were needed! (…) There is a sort of complicity, an attachment, a sensitivity between the grape-grower and his vine, or the wine-maker and his wine, an awareness that is very specific to viticulture, due to the age-old cultivation of the crop, the care it needs, the tailoring of the product and its role in society (…) Phylloxera destroyed this emotional balance, depriving the wine-maker (…) of the moral resources needed for swift rebuilding'.

Crises are character-building and weld together the active elements in a community. The few inhabitants of Tavel who devoted themselves to the rebuilding of the vineyard proved their solidarity. Self-help was mutualised. In 1887, the local council voted in a loan of one thousand francs to purchase 10,000 American seedlings, the only ones resistant to the insect. These were made available gratis to grape-growers. For obvious reasons, neither migration of the vineyards to soil consisting of pure sand, as in the Camargue and the Landes, nor their immersion under water for several weeks proved to be a possibility in Tavel. Treatment with an insecticide such as potassium sulphocarbonate was also impractical, as it was so laborious to apply that only a few of the great Crus Classés of Médoc could afford it. Vine stocks were multiplied, cuttings were taken, there were graftings. On the eve of World War I, Tavel's vines barely covered 195 hectares. By 1926, they had reached 260, covering 300 hectares in the 1930s, but they were own again to 275 hectares in 1952.

Behind this hesitant growth there was also a will that was not always evident but that has paid off – that of following the quality route. The grape-grower and wine-making has had only two solutions available to him since the dawn of time. He can either plant and harvest a maximum and sell at a lower price in order to beat the competition, or harvest a smaller amount of a higher quality and sell at the highest price. In order to make the latter choice, he needs to have a strong, well-founded and long-lasting reputation. In Tavel there was little choice. The sandy terroir was not very fertile, the land strewn with pebbles and limestone rocks was even poorer, so competition for high yield was simply not an option. Thanks to the centuries-old reputation of the village, the inhabitants staked all on the quality of their product and added 'making known' to their ancestral know-how, at the cost of a slow recovery. After all, following an absence of several decades, they not only had to replant but had to regain the markets. This, while protecting themselves from fraud and passing-off of a name 'that resonates', as Monique Fraissinet puts it, she being one of the last people to witness the slow but fundamental revival of Tavel wine-making.

Throughout Europe, during the second half of the nineteenth century, the small growers organised themselves by forming unions to defend themselves, central purchasing schemes and even the first cooperative cellars in Germany, Switzerland and Spain. In France, a law permitting the creation of a union was passed in March 1884. But French viticulture was slow to organise. The first wine-makers' unions did not emerge until the very beginning of the twentieth century. At Chablis in Burgundy, 79 owners gathered together in order to guarantee 'the authenticity of the wines and grouping all the vine owners together to facilitate the sale of their products'. In Bordeaux the *Union syndicale des propriétaires de Crus Classés du Médoc* was created, now known as the *Conseil des Grands Crus Classés en 1855.*

The people of Tavel were not slow to follow suit and in 1902 –and this time long before their neighbours – they formed a syndicate of owner-growers, whose purpose could not have been clearer, namely: 'To guarantee the authenticity of

the wines of Tavel; to keep the consumer informed of the quantities produced and to suppress fraud through every means'. The syndicate's 59 members included the mayor and two château owners – there appeared to be total unity.

The French government supported efforts at protection of agricultural produce through passing various laws. That of 1 August 1905 marked the beginning of the *appellations d'origine* that we know today, followed and supplemented by the law of 6 May 1919 that made it possible to delineate a production area by getting a court order and finally that of 22 July 1927, which included 'local, loyal and constant' production usages (see Marcel Lachiver). The various laws of 1907, voted in hastily after the rebellion of the wine-makers of Languedoc which Clémenceau suppressed with an iron fist, introduced the declaration of the harvest and stocks and the fight to combat fraud, with the creation of the suppression of fraud and the decree that defined wine as being the 'exclusive result of alcoholic fermentation of the fresh grape or fresh grape juice' (see Marcel Lachiver).

Tavel's efforts in this respect, which led the movement in the département, received the support of Senator Méjean who 'wanted his département to have at least one cru classé' (see Jacques Maby) as well as by Baron Le Roy, a jurist and wine-maker from Châteauneuf-du-Pape who, in 1923, founded the syndicate of Châteauneuf grape-growers, twenty years after that of Tavel.

Fortified by this support and the legal provisions

that defined the legislative context, the people of Tavel started legal proceedings against the owners of vineyards who appeared to be usurping the name of Tavel. In order to be able to cover the costs of the law suit, the syndicate asked for a loan from the Crédit Agricole bank. This was refused due to the absence of sufficient guarantees. The people of Tavel learned their lesson and asked for another loan in order to buy pesticides, and this time it was granted. Thanks to this wily, peasant subterfuge, the way was now clear for action in the courts.

It is important to understand that the people of Tavel never intended to enter into combat with unscrupulous wine-makers. They were seeking much more. They had decided to obtain, and even force through a landmark case. Thus, Jacques Maby recounts that the syndicate was even seeking to prosecute 'opponents who merely complied and who were charged with claiming the right to the Tavel appellation in terroirs that were too damp or in a neighbouring village'.

On 6 November, 1928, Aimé Roudil, president of the grape-growing syndicate, gathered all the members together and read to them 'from a telegram announcing the happy news that the law suit for the delimitation of our grand cru has been upheld by the Nîmes Court of Appeal. (…) The Baron Le Roy was unanimously acclaimed honorary president of our syndicate, due to his devotion to defending our cause (…)' (Extract from the minutes of the extraordinary session, archives from the Tavel syndicate).

Tavel thus became the first wine-producing district to benefit from the legal provisions that defined an *appellation d'origine*. Châteauneuf-du-

larger ones – the cooperative cellar soon became one of the pillars of quality for the wines of Tavel. Tavel wine sold well and things continued to go well even during the economic downturn of the first decade of the second millennium. Tavel is currently getting ready, without denying its origins, to win over new consumers, from the youngest French people to enthusiasts for new export markets.

Tavel therefore has every right to claim the designation as being the leading rosé in France. It has the right historically and legally. Except for the fact that rosé has never actually been produced in Tavel, not in the past and not today. Tavel wine is 'a red wine the colour of rubies tinted with gold' as stated in a document dating from the start of the century. But since this description is legally the default, the people of Tavel have resigned themselves, like it or not, to using the term 'rosé', a term which in any case only dates from the mid-nineteenth century and whose description, and even its legal protection, remains vague at the risk of it being confused with 'true' rosés from here or from elsewhere. If, from the official creation of the Tavel appellation to the present day, and despite the fact that the terroir of the appellation is also usable for the production of quality red wines – and why not even white wines? – the local wine-makers have voluntarily restricted themselves to the colour of the historic red wines that predated the conquest of the world by darker-coloured wines. They ought to have good reason to do so, and each Tavel native mentions his or her own. They include respect for past achievements, the special nature of the original terroir in sandy soil that indeed favoured the creation of light red wines, too much competition in the market for dark red wines, a deep-seated rejection of wine that was too brightly coloured which was the cause of the Phylloxera catastrophe and many more. Let us simply hail the foresight or instinct for survival of the founders of the appellation who understood long before its time that white wine, red wine and especially rosé wine can be produced anywhere in the world, but Tavel wine can only be made in Tavel.

Pape followed suit a year later. In 1935, after the creation of the Comité National des Appellations d'Origine (which in 1947 became the Institut National des Appellations d'Origine), Tavel became of the first *crus* to claim this new status. On 15 May 1936, Cognac, the district that produced brandy, and four wine-making *crus* were granted the status of an Appellation d'Origine Contrôlée. These were Arbois in the Jura, Châteauneuf, Tavel and Cassis in the French Midi.

During the twentieth century, the *cru* status of Côtes-du-Rhône enabled Tavel to reconstitute its original vineyard and even expand it, adding the land of the limestone *lauses* of Vestides, west of the village. In 1938, the cooperative cellar was inaugurated by the then president of the French Republic. By absorbing the production of the 'small' grape-growers – as well as that of a few

THE TERROIR

Ever since grapes were first grown in the Lower Languedoc (and elsewhere), vines have been grown for preference on the lower slopes or in foothills close to human habitation, unlike more fertile land that is reserved for food crops or animal husbandry. Vines were generally cultivated on gentle slopes that were less subject to erosion or on terraces dug out by human hands. If vine seedlings are to grow normally, they need regular, controlled watering if they are to produce quality grapes. Consequently, they require well-drained soils, capable of remaining damp enough so that they can feed the plant during periods of drought. The optimum maturity of the grape is achieved thanks to natural sunlight that is sufficiently abundant in the département of Gard. This maturing is often reinforced by nights that are frequently cool or periods of strong winds and soils that contain pebbles or limestone rocks that reflect the sun's heat. Not only are the two dominant winds, the Mistral and the Tramontane, cooling, they also ventilate the vines, clear the atmosphere and dry out the leaves and bunches of grapes after summer storms that are often violent. Both these winds are thus considered as valuable allies for the grape-grower who wants to work as naturally as possible and who seeks to treat his crop only when the pressure of fungus diseases leaves him little choice.

In the days when land was cultivated with a plough drawn by horses or oxen, the vineyards were confined to land that could be easily ploughed and any cultivation on slopes that were too steep or plots of land with sub-soil that was too stony were excluded. Thus, the vineyard of Tavel originally developed in its lowest area, known as l'Olivet or le Plan, to the east and north of the village. It is on these sandy soils dotted with pebbles and clay that a few of the historic estates of Tavel can be found. These include Château Manissy, Château d'Aquéria, Château de Trinquevedel and Château de

Montézargues. Laater, as the vineyard expanded at the end of the seventeenth century until it was destroyed by phylloxera, the grape-growers of Tavel conquered the stony ground that was cultivatable situated on the Villafranchian terrace of Vallongue, north of the village, and the limestone soils of Vestides, in the west.

Then along came phylloxera and almost entirely wiped out the vineyard. The true recovery of the abandoned terroirs did not begin until the mid-twentieth century, in the 1950s. There was a consolidation and a limited amount of grape-growing land was made available, slightly expanding beyond the area to land that had never been planted with vines in the past. With the help of powerful mechanical earth-movers, the people of Tavel were able to clear away all the pebbles and extend their vines over the major part of the limestone *lauses* of the Vestides. It is this triptych of terroirs, l'Olivet or le Plan, Vallongue and les Vestides, in an area ranging from 50 to 200 metres above sea level and covering around a thousand hectares, that produces the Tavel wine of today.

In Tavel, the various types of soil definitely affect the style of the wines made from the grapes harvested from them. This is the result not of their chemical composition – for soil, like money, has no smell! – but due to the way they are constituted physiologically, their ability to regulate their water intake and how the seedling is fed, as well as their microbial fauna, as long as this is allowed to express itself without the massive addition of artificial fertiliser or worse synthetic weed-killers and insecticides.

The wines made from grapes grown on sandy soils are often the finest, they are lightest in alcohol and with a strong bouquet and, as an accident of the climate, the yields from these soils are often higher. The stony soil confers a more powerful and vinous character to the Tavel, where as the limestone lauses are more unforgiving, with low yields, although the produce wines of character and with an unusual minerality.

Due to land being divided up through inheritance and despite the consolidation of the 1950s, the map of the plots of Tavel vineyard is once again very dispersed and currently almost all of the estates own vines growing on several types of soil. Tavel is thus one of those blended wines, a *vin d'assemblage*, like claret or champagne.

THE SANDS

Vincent de Bez, co-owner with his brother of the Château d'Aquéria, a handsome property surrounded by vines at the lowest part of the Tavel vineyard, mentioned to us that 'the sand of our soils is nothing like the sand on a beach'. In fact, it can be seen that this type of Pliocene sand is quite rare, even in the region, although a little can be found at Roquemaure, Domazan, Estézargues and in the south-east of the Costières de Nîmes (see Jacques Maby). This soil is workable enough to be cultivatable without causing problems, but it is very poor in organic matter. The visible part consists of yellow, acid and decarbonated coarse sand and a few pebbles that have rolled down from the surrounding Villafranchian terraces.

At a slightly greater depth, from about 30 centimetres, a few residues of clay are added, probably resulting from an older soil. The bedrock lies sixty centimetres down; it consists

of compressed Pliocene sands and non-decarbonated limestone sands.

The soil is therefore quite cool and filtering but slightly fearful of drought. The vines are forced to develop an extensive root system, guaranteeing varied feeding with trace elements – always on condition that the plants are only fed measured amounts of natural fertiliser. This favours the development of precursors of aroma, as well as slow and progressive maturing, due to the relatively dry soil. In my professional experience which, it should be admitted, is much more empirical than scientific, this type of soil does not produce wines with any great tannic strength. At optimal maturity in relation to the development of aroma, the acidity remains quite high. Consequently, in this climate area and altitude, a sandy soil such as this is mostly suited to the production of white wines, supple and tender red wines or rosés. This original terroir therefore does not enable the production of wines of a deeper colour, thus providing an

de Nîmes most of which are rightly claimed to be in the latter district. Residues of these terraces also emerge near Lirac and Estezargues. These are fluvial deposits that were compressed by the river Rhone in the Quaternary era and that created the Alps. Seventy-five per cent of the soil consists of large, rounded pebbles, between ten and forty centimetres in diameter, as smooth and silky as a precious stone. They are reddish and ochre in colour and are mixed with whole blocks of stone and quartz sand. The layer of pebbles is generally between five and fifteen metres in depth but it can be as much as 40 metres thick in Costières. The stones are sometimes flanked or even mixed with or covered with more recent strata of alluvial soil (see Jacques Maby).

This desert of tightly packed stones which is much more impressive than the sandy soils, in which even weeds struggle to grow, stores solar heat which it released during the night. The topsoil covered with smooth pebbles ensures good drainage, except in places unsuitable for vines where the clay residues plug any gaps, rendering the soil almost waterproof. These soils also fear drought and favour the development of an extensive root system. In this task the vine is helped by human intervention, using the 1.50 metre teeth of a bulldozer to break up the sub-soil to quite a depth, facilitating the penetration of roots and rootlets. This means that the soils not only guarantee optimal maturity and thus good resorption of the acidity, but they also are able to store sugar and create thick skins that are rich in polyphenols and colouring matter. This is the favourite terroir for generous, heady wines. if, for a short period in its long history, Tavel was able to produce red wines of a deeper colour – and according to certain sources this happened just before the phylloxera plague, perhaps to follow the fashion of the time (see the history on pages 34-35) – these must have been produced from grapes harvested from this terroir rather than from the sandy soils. The round pebbles confer upon today's Tavel body, alcoholic strength, structure and keeping qualities.

additional reason for the historical production of rosé or pale red wines in Tavel.

Tavel wines and Tavel blended wines produced solely from these terroirs, derive all their finesse and elegance from this soil type.

The smooth pebbles

The section of vineyard known as Vallongue is an integral part of the Villafranchian terraces that stretch from Châteauneuf-du-Pape to Costières

THE LAUSES

This third type of soil was harder to conquer and remains the most arduous to cultivate. Yet it may be the one that is most influential in the expression of the Tavel wine of today. The soil covered in limestone rocks known as *lauses* in the Vestides district, of which only a very small part was planted out in the 'good old days', was mostly annexed in the 1960s and 1970s. It made the region famous as 'Tavel stone', a high-quality material used for construction and decoration, and still being sold by the Tavel marble works. The *lauses* cover an area of just over 300 hectares, constituting the most arid and poorest soil in Tavel. Water and nutrients are rare on the surface, and it is not surprising to find the remains of irrigation pipes used for planting vines. Here again the plants are forced to create a deep and extensive root system.

The *lauses* terroir was finally cleared through a titanic struggle. As for the smooth pebbles, heavy machinery was used to break up the top layer, 60% of which consisted of limestone rocks mixed with silt and clay. At a depth of thirty centimetres, 90% of the soil consists of rocky debris and marly limestone, supplemented by a few pockets of clay. The limestone bedrock which is solid and slightly cracked begins at a depth of sixty centimetres.

I assume that this type of soil that is extremely mineral might also produce particularly highly concentrated white wines – since the yields are often derisory. The grapes grown here today produce dense, taut rosés, high in minerals, of a rare finesse and a particularly fruity aroma. When blended, wines from the *lauses* constitute the ideal complement for the creation of a complex wine with a unique character.

In order to better express the complexity of the soils, the Tavel wine-maker has patiently selected a wide palette of stocks from among the varieties grown in the region, choosing those that are best suited to the styles and terroirs of Tavel.

THE GRAPE STOCKS

The Tavel wine-makers have always created their wines by giving themselves the option of using a large number of vine stocks, both red and white, and thus resisting the temptation for the uniformity that is all the rage in our gardens, fields and vineyards. The decree issued by Tavel stipulating that no vine stock in the Tavel vineyard must cover more than 60% of the area of a plot has barred the way to any 'vine-stock monomania'. Yet in the last few decades, the veteran wine-makers have made some concession to the current trend by restricting their choice to the main, best known and most easily cultivatable stocks. The demands put upon them to adapt to a changing climate that is becoming hotter and drier could bring back into favour certain varieties that have been slightly neglected.

The indisputable basis for all Tavel wine is Red Grenache, the king stock of the South. It is often supplemented by Mourvèdre, which contributes more structure and a slight spiciness, and especially by Cinsault, which for a time was unfairly neglected, but which is now being planted to an increasing extent, since it is suitable for the production of aromatic rosés full of finesse. Grenache gives Tavel wine its general expression, its warmth, fruitiness and roundness. Carignan, when grown at suitable exposures and under controlled yield conditions, but which has rightly been accused of having a certain robustness, gives Tavel rosé greater structure and body. Syrah is still very fashionable virtually everywhere in the South of France, gives the wine the fragrance of berries, raspberries and strawberries, and even of acid drops, a flavour very sought after in contemporary rosés. The same is true of Bourboulenc, a white or pink Clairette, an interesting stock to rediscover which adds more elegance, suppleness and a certain freshness during blending. Calitor and Picpoul, in white or red, complete this extensive and interesting palette.

Red Grenache

Grenache stock originates from span where it is known as Aragones or Alicante (Cannonau in Sardinia and Elegante in Corsica). It produces compact bunches of large to medium size, with juicy grapes whose skin is quite thick and whose pulp is melting. It buds relatively early, is quite drought-resistant and its branches can withstand even quite violent winds. It is not sensitive to oidium wilt, but is more susceptible to mildew, grey mould (*Botrytis cinerea*) and grape worms. It likes a sunny exposure on a slope or foothill and appreciates well-drained soils, even those that are dry, arid and stony. It is thus perfectly suited to the terroirs of Tavel, where it is not that productive but generally produces wines of very high quality. The Grey and White Grenache varieties, also permitted under the Tavel appellation are now only rarely cultivated.

Cinsault

At one time, this stock was very widespread in the French Midi, but it was abandoned in favour of certain more fashionable varieties such as Syrah. It produces large compact bunches of large, firm, juicy grapes that are blue-black in colour. It buds late, so it is quite a fragile stock, of average vigour but very sensitive to fungal diseases and parasites. If the yield is controlled, it produces quite warm wines but ones that are supple and less tannic than those made from Grenache, Mourvèdre or Carignan, with delicious aromas reminiscent of fresh almonds. It is thus the ideal complement for the making of Tavel rosé.

MOURVÈDRE

Mourvèdre is known as Spar or Espar in Languedoc and Monastrell in Spain. It is a classic stock of the South, and is one of the foundations for the great red wines of Bandol. It produces average sized compact bunches of small grapes whose flesh is melting and whose skin is thick. It buds and matures late, but does not like frost so it requires a warm exposure. It is also quite sensitive to oidium wilt and mildew, and has a low yield. The wines made from it are tannic and acrid, less hardy than those made from Carignan, but they contribute structure to Tavel and improve its keeping qualities.

CARIGNAN

Often described as hardy, Carignan comes from ancient stock with a derisorily low yield but grown in certain locations it can produce some very interesting wines. This vigorous vine buds and matures early but is very susceptible to oidium wilt and mildew. It produces quite large bunches of average-sized grapes whose juice is rather pallid but it has a thick skin with a slightly astringent taste. The stock is limited to 10% in Tavel so as to mitigate any coarseness, but it contributes a certain harshness and thus greater structure, and even a pleasant hint of bitterness.

Syrah

Syrah has come south from north of the Rhône, and has been planted more extensively in Provence and Languedoc since the 1950s. It remains a very fashionable stock. This variety buds quite late but matures slightly earlier than the vine stocks previously discussed. It produces medium-sized bunches with small, melting grapes having a very fruity taste. The skin is thin but very resistant. In Tavel, it is slightly susceptible to drought. With its delightful notes of raspberry and strawberry, and even of redcurrant, elderberry and blackcurrant, it contributes a trendy note to Tavel.

Clairette

This ancient white vine stock is used to produce dry white wines in Languedoc and the southern Rhône valley, especially at Bellegarde (Clairette de Bellegarde). This variety was ignored for a while in favour of more aromatic stocks such as Rolle or Viognier. Today, Clairette is experienced a certain rehabilitation, if a hesitant one, in the South of France. The bunches are medium to large, not very compact and consist of medium-sized, juicy, firm grapes that are white with brown patches. This plant buds and matures late, but grows vigorously and likes arid, dry soils, making it sensitive to mildew and oidium. The branches do not hold up well in strong winds. Wines based on Clairette oxidise a little too easily, but if the yields are controlled it can contribute a certain suppleness to Tavel wine, as well as floral and subtly spiced notes of dried fruits. It is thus very suitable for Tavel wines that seek a more expressive bouquet.

Bourboulenc

This white vintage which retains its acidity even in a sunny position is the ideal complement for any Tavel wine. This hardy and vigorous stock buds quite early, producing average-sized bunches whose white, average-sized grapes are white tinged with pink. Bourboulenc is sensitive to oidium wilt, and generally requires late harvesting. It then expresses itself in delicious floral aromas and a fine fresh texture.

Piquepoul

This variety exists in white, red and grey. It was once very common around the basin of the river Thau where it was used for making vermouth. It is still the basis for the white wine known as Piquepoul de Pinet. It has been in decline for several years, even in Tavel. It develops bunches of average size whose juicy grapes have thin skins. It buds late and is susceptible to grey mould and oidium. Piquepoul produces wines that are high in alcohol but it retains its acidity well and contributes pleasant floral and fruit fragrances to the blend.

CALITOR

This ancient black variety, which was once very common in Provence, is hardy and produces well. It is rather picky about the choice of soil and exposure, but it has proved to be quite resistant to phylloxera. In its best exposures, Calitor, which is hardly grown any more in Tavel, can produce pallid wines though ones with a certain finesse (see Pierre Galet, *Dictionnaire Encyclopédique des Cépages*, Hachette, 2000).

Techniques and Vinification

The historic vineyard favours the collective conscience and is the vehicle for an ancestral know-how transmitted from father to son and very happily, and more and more frequently, from father or mother to daughter. This particular advantage may also reveal itself to be a disadvantage, however, since tradition can very soon become a considerable burden, a yoke around the neck of young people who, while aware of local custom and usage, are also amenable to the progress necessary if there is to be any development.

It is interesting to observe that in Tavel, the role of grandfathers is often more important than that of fathers. It is the grandfather who contributes from a recent past in which neither artificial fertiliser nor insecticides nor chemical weed-killers existed, nor were there these gigantic, very heavy tractors and earth-movers, just a few simple tools such as the hoe and the plough; the only treatment was Bordeaux mixture. Tavel is in the process of turning itself into a stronghold of organic viticulture as a result of this pact between the two generations, in which hard work is once again replacing non-cultivation – isn't 'non-cultivation' the right work to describe the abandonment of working the soil in favour of herbicides? – where natural products are supplanting the miraculous pharmacy of agrochemistry. Although these generations may be separated by age, they are very close in their way of thinking. Of course organics are all the rage and have become an irrefutable sales pitch but here again the reasons for the choice do not matter, environmentally-friendly viticulture benefits everyone.

A vineyard that is chemically weeded, leaving not even a vestige of microbial life and soil compacted by heavy machinery, simply cannot produce grapes suitable for making a wine with even a semblance of expression of the terroir. If you want to exterminate weeds like this, why not grow grapes without any soil? Nourishing – and watering – the world isn't simple. I am not accusing industrial viticulture of anything,

it advertises itself as such and it has its own *raison d'être*, but Tavel will never be part of it since neither its size nor its terroir would make this possible. Of course, a small estate whose owner works his vineyard himself and does not count the time he spends would be easier to manage than a huge spread with a workforce that needs to be paid, but the consumer will be happy to cover the extra cost if the final result is worth it. We can do nothing more than to support the efforts of the leaders of Tavel who affirm with ever greater vigour their reversion to responsible viticulture.

There is nothing slapdash about working in this way, quite the opposite. It requires more care, vigilance, accuracy and adaptation to each case. The processes described here are merely there to outline a way of working that each grape-grower and wine-maker adapts to his or her own case, their own experience, with the assistance of an œnologist or advice from family members or neighbours with whom they discuss their problems.

In Tavel, as elsewhere, the priority to obtain perfectly healthy raw materials. The grape-grower who harvests his perfectly ripe – but not overripe! – grapes that are consistent but have no astringency, is already two-thirds of the way to a unique, high-quality product. Thanks to the hard work of the people of Tavel, this is mostly the case.

The growers of Tavel are well supported by modern technology which attempts to replace chemicals, wherever possible, by physical processes. They prefer to harvest during the cooler periods of the day, often early in the morning, and do so manually or mechanically with a carefully adjusted harvesting machine. They then transport the grapes with care, often in crates. They must remain as intact as possible, and reach the cellar very quickly where the harvest is immediately chilled. That way, it will not suffer any deterioration, any wild, premature fermentation.

After being lightly crushed, the bunches of

grapes are transferred whole to the vat, without de-stemming, then the bunches are broken down. The wine-maker places the harvest in the vat, either variety by variety or plot by plot, assembled or pre-assembled. This maceration phase de prior to cold fermentation makes it possible to extract the primary floral and fruit aromas, the tannins and colorants.

The grape is generally macerated for between 12 and 48 hours, or even slightly longer, depending on the type of wine and the colour desired. This maceration is performed at temperature oscillating between a maximum of 10 to 15 degrees Celsius in order to inhibit any unwanted fermentation. Tavel wine being above all a maceration rosé – or a pale red wine – this phase thus proves to be of crucial importance and one that is absolutely vital.

The Tavel wine-maker then proceeds to a *saignée*, a 'bleeding' that consists in separating the liquids from the solids and/or pressing the solids. The use of ultra-accurate modern pneumatic presses makes it possible to obtain a pressed juice of the finest quality. Very often the juice exuded naturally and the pressed juice and vinified separately and assembled at a later stage. Alcoholic fermentation is then triggered, either with the help of selected yeasts, or using natural yeasts from the product. In both these cases, the temperature needs to remain relatively low, within a range of between 13 and 15 degrees minimum and 20 to 22 degrees maximum. Malolactic fermentation, which is largely inhibited, may be triggered once alcoholic fermentation has been completed.

Bottling is generally performed five or six months after the harvest, using bottles that are generally stamped with the official initials of the appellation after batches or blends have been selected. This phase of wine-making almost always takes place in vats, very rarely in barrels or casks, is absolutely necessary for making Tavel wine more supple since, it should again be remembered it is much more like a rich red wine but a supple one with a pale tint.

Once it has been bottled, Tavel is ready to be tasted for our greater pleasure. But to make it even better, it will gain from waiting two or three months, or even longer. In any case every wine-making will be glad to tell you the right time for drinking his or her Tavel, which is generally between nine and eighteen months after the harvest.

SECOND PART ESTATES AND WINE-MAKERS

The following pages contain thirty-seven portraits of all the caves and all the independent wine-producers, as well as the Cave des Vignerons de Tavel and the Cave de Roquemaure which also vinifies wine in Tavel, both of which produce excellent wines! Each grower or manager participated in an interview lasting about ten minutes in which he or she explained how they viewed and how they made Tavel wine. I have tried to retranscribe these contributions as faithfully as possible. My comments are merely beacons to guide you, where necessary, along the path of initiation through the various styles and personalities of Tavel wine. Initially, they will also help you to choose the dish to accompany the wine or the most appropriate times to drink it. But do not forget that Tavel wine is a wine that provides freedom to act and think, wine that takes responsibility for its and it emancipated, recognising no restrictions!

Domaine Amido
DREAM TEAM

Nathalie Patinet
Antoine Berthaud
Amandine Patinet
Dominique Le Dantec

'Our father, Christian Amido, created his own plot in 1987. In 2000, he was able to make his dream come true, that of creating his own cellar. The estate originates from the Maby estate, once owned and managed by my grandfather. We took it over in 2003, after my father's death. We mainly produce Tavel wine, as well as a little Lirac, Pays d'Oc wine and, as the result of purchasing five hectares at Rochefort-du-Gard, some Côtes-du-Rhône Villages.

I deal with the accounts and with the customers, my sister Dominique is the wine-maker. She was a computer programmer in Paris, but she was glad to leave the capital to return to Tavel when it became necessary. My daughter Amandine whose first name has been given to our Tavel has also joined us, as well as her friend Antoine, who is in charge of the cellar. We are a real family estate.

Our spread covers 27 hectares and four communes, enabling us to offer a complete range to our customers. Most of our vines are actually located in Tavel, however, and on the three terroirs, where we carefully nurture five of the nine varieties that make up the cru. These are Grenache, Cinsault, Syrah, Clairette and Carignan. This mixture gives our Tavel all of its complexity. We operate environmentally-friendly farming, of the type known in France as *culture raisonnée*, but we dream of one day becoming organic and working our soils mechanically so that we no longer need to use defoliants.

Les Amandines, the cuvee we produce is a Tavel rosé *par excellence*. It is both structured and well-bred, with deep, fruity aromas and a pleasantly round, refreshing finale, complex in its blending of the five varieties. It is a rosé that can be drunk as an aperitive or to accompany a meal.

We are trying to remain faithful to the expression of the terroir, but sometimes a more fruity note and a more structured, tannic note must be contributed. Nothing is every set in stone. One year we will look for greater freshness, another year more roundness or fruitiness.

We are always able to develop. Previously, when the temperature of the maceration could not be controlled, it easily rose to 25 degrees. With the change in mentalities and the influx of young people, tastes have changed. Today, the market is asking us to produce rosés that are more fruity and supple. This means that a technological aspect needs to be taken into account during vinification. This is where youth intervenes, young people vinify for the tastes of today. The typicality of Tavel still needs to be respected of course, its colour and structure remain important.

We are three women here. Things are not always easy. We are 'only' women. But we don't dwell on the fact. We contribute our touch of femininity without giving ourselves a complex. Things are changing. Women involved in wine-making is very trendy. We are starting to be taken seriously.

Is Tavel a masculine wine? Not here! Ever since we took over the estate, our wines have become more fruity, more supple, finer, and the colour is not so dark. Without completely changing the style defined by our father, we are making a Tavel that happens to please ourselves. That way, we are sure it will please others'.

It is certainly pleasing – it pleases us, for one thing! This Tavel is made by two generations of a family working hand-in-hand. It has deliciously fruity and green almond notes and it is well-balanced without heaviness. Les Amandines cuvee can be drunk as an aperitive, served slightly colder than is customary, or a normal temperature – remember Tavel best reveals its potential at between 12 °C and 14 °C! – to accompany a Camargue-style tomato risotto.

Le palai nord
Route de la commanderie
30126 Tavel
Tel.: +33 (0)4 66 50 04 41
E-mail: domaineamido@cegetel.fr

L'Anglore
IGNORE THE DENIGRATION

Eric Pfifferling

'I manage a family property which has expanded since my arrival in 1988, when I took over the running. It consists of eight hectares of vines, five of them in Tavel, with some in Côtes-du-Rhône and in Coteaux-du-Languedoc. Until 2001, I brought my harvest to the Tavel cooperative cellar which I regretfully left, in order to pursue my reasoning to the ultimate, for which purpose I needed to vinify my grapes independently. Today, the estate employs four people, all the production is organic and we have biological culture certification. The main grape stock we grow is Grenache, supplemented by the classic varieties of the appellation.

Hard to believe, but an eight-hectare vineyard is a big machine! My aim is to be able to stabilise the ship, but the time taken to make wine does not match that of the economy. We spend time and money preparing the soil and tending the vines, without mentioning the wine-making, bottling and marketing. We take it all on ourselves, from A to Z.

The purchase by the consumer of a bottle of wine produced organically is an action undertaken in defence of viticulture on a human scale. Tavel is an appellation that does well in terms of organic culture. More than a dozen grape-growers and wine-makers are operating organically or are in the process of being converted.

Personally, I have always defended diversity, I have never allowed the estate to denigrate others. I have always acted as an ambassador for my appellation even though certain people accuse me of having defended my own property first, but it could not exist if the appellation didn't exist!

I am fed by the collective memory of this village, I have tried to think and gather evidence from the old people, I wanted to know how this wine was made fifty years ago. It shouldn't be forgotten that rosé is a recent fashion, a wine without a true history. We originally made claret in Tavel, that is to say, light red wines. Our wine-making culture gradually collapsed, whole generations were raised in acquiescence. They didn't ask too many questions. They followed the fashions.

In an appellation such as Tavel, history is important, we owe it a debt and need to continue what it started. When we have gone Tavel wine will remain and people will retain the history and the tradition. That is what gives it its strength. The œnology of the past thirty years has been important for correcting a certain amount of deviation, but it has also lowered the bar. We don't make bad wine today, far from it, but it is being standardised. But I remain confident. A dynamic is being introduced and the younger generation of vine-growers and wine-makers are discovering and appropriating indigenous yeasts that originate from the terroir – the real thing – and finding out the singular nature they give the wines. Impossible to mention the terroir without speaking of respect for these native yeasts for they provide the bloom on which the whole family of yeasts is deposited. Yeast is the cornerstone of wine of the terroir'.

Eric, a star of wine?
Don't ever call him that, he would never forgive you. He just wants to be considered as a conscientious wine-maker, that's all. His wine is a dark ruby colour – darker than the other Tavel wine. It is also more vinous, a real pale red, with structure and taste, a Tavel that revives past memories, interpreted in a contemporary way by an exceptional wine-maker, heir to the elders of Tavel such as Brother Roger de Manissy and Monique Fraissinet whom he patiently questioned at length. Eric is thoughtful and resolute, even revolutionary in the way he sees and interprets wine, but he remains 100% a Tavel native in his soul as well as in his actions, and an ardent defender of the appellation.

L'Anglore
Route du Vignoble
30126 Tavel
Tel.: +33 (0)4 66 33 08 46
E-mail: anglore@wanadoo.fr

Château d'Aquéria
Noblesse oblige

Vincent de Bez

'Our estate owes its name to the Marquis d'Aquéria de Rochegude who in 1575 purchased from the monks of the Abbey of Villeneuve-Lès-Avignon the land known as *puy sablonneux* (sandhill). He began to clear it and to build a house that gradually became a manor house. It was not until 1725 that the château was born. The ruins of Gallo-Roman villas are evidence of a long grape-growing tradition on the property which really got going in the eighteenth century. At the time, true Tavel was not sold because the appellation has only existed since the beginning of the twentieth century, and anyway rosé was completely unknown. The only distinction was between red and white wine. The wines produced here were pale red in colour, as were most of the crus at that time. Over the centuries, the Château d'Aquéria changed owners several times.

Our grandfather, Jean-Olivier, who was born in Avignon, owned an orchard at Saint-Rémy-de-Provence and purchased the estate in 1919. I now manage it with my brother Bruno, and we represent the third generation on site. With its 100 hectares of land, of which 70 hectares consist of vineyard of virtually a single type surrounding the château and its sandhill, d'Aquéria is one of the largest estates in the appellation.

The sand of our soils is nothing like the sand on a beach. It is mixed with clay and large pebbles and it filters well, thus avoiding excess humidity which would harm the vine. On the other hand, it suffers in a drought due to its capillarity, dampness in the sub-soil can penetrate the roots of the stock.

Vincent de Bez enjoys enabling us to discover a timeless wine that seems in itself to summarise the whole history of Tavel. It is fruity and fresh, of course, and consequently, totally contemporary. It also has a rare depth and complexity. It deserves to be drunk after being allowed to rest for one or even two years in a cellar and then decanted into a carafe. Serve it as an aperitive so as to be able to fully benefit from its rare balance, or simply accompanied by a few tapas, such as pieces of toasts spread with tapenade, bread topped with tomates or slices of the local charcuterie.

The many trees growing on our property create a very special microclimate. The d'Aquéria Tavel is taken from this terroir, which produces a fruity wine, a rich one of course, but one that has good acidity that gives it freshness.

The future of our appellation is based on respect for the terroir and our most important role consists in promoting its richness in order to allow it to express itself in all its splendour by using most of the grape stocks of the appellation. The future thus passes through the quality of our work, the upkeep of our vineyard and enhancing the landscape in a region in which we are the envy of visitors from everywhere in Europe. It is our duty to ensure that this cultural and environmental heritage lives up to the standard of our wines'.

Château d'Aquéria
30126 Tavel
Tel.: +33 (0) 466 50 04 56
E-mail: contact@aqueria.com
Website: www.aqueria.com

Domaine Beaumont
Leaving so as to better return

Brice Beaumont

Domaine Beaumont
Chemin de la Filature
30126 Lirac
Tel.: +33 (0)4 66 50 02 37
E-mail: domainebeaumont@wanadoo.fr

'Our vineyard was created in 1909 by my great-grandfather, David. You can see him here in this photograph, next to me. I started living here in 2001, after studying œnology and spending some time in the United States, in the State of Oregon to be exact, where I worked for a while on the Drouhin estate. I was happy to leave, to see something else and discover new horizons. I approached another way of considering wine and talking about it. By keeping out of the way, I was afraid I would ossify.

But I was very glad to be back. I am from Gard, I have my roots here, I love my land, my culture. When I left Oregon I felt some twinges but at the same time I was happy to come home to put into practice what I had learned over there, with all that my father handed down to me to try and produce the product I believe in.

Our estate is in Lirac. We produce three appellations: Tavel, Lirac and Côtes-du-Rhône. For our Tavel wine, we cultivate a small plot at the entrance to Vallongue and at the edge of the Vaussière, plateau. The soil has a clay base and smooth pebbles, which gives the wine spicy notes and a nice structure, fruitiness and substance. We are thus a classic of the cru.

We make our Tavel from a small plot, using varieties that are typical of the South – Grenache, Cinsault, Carignan, Mourvèdre and a few white stocks. This cannot be learned anywhere else but here locally. But the wine can be improved and this is where my stay in the United States comes in and my confrontation with other points of view.

I start out from the principle that once can have innovative ideas without having to cut oneself off from one's roots. It's like a vine plant, if you cut off the roots it will die.

I am one of the younger generation of vine-growers – whether they belong to a cooperative cellar or a private cellar – who are interested in what is happening elsewhere. This means we can get the best out of each world. By retaining what works well for us, we can incorporate other techniques, both in vinification, working the land and marketing our product. That way, Tavel wine has a bright future ahead of it.

In recent-years we were not always in the pink (it has to be said), but we really have huge potential. We can feel the market beginning to quake, the rosé axis becoming a profitable one, and not a mere fleeting, seasonal fashion. It is a product that is sustainable. The structure, texture and body of Tavel can take full advantage of this tendency, since it is enjoyed in summer by the pool as much as in winter at the fireside.

My dream? To be able to keep the estate going in the long run and developing my export network further. I want us to belong to the estates that count'.

Brice's wine bears the hallmark of an experienced wine-maker, you can feel the hand of an experienced wine-maker at work, whose technical skill results in a cleanliness and precision that are rare, even in Tavel, without denying the origins of the wine. With its handsome aromatic expression of flowers and fruit, its elegance and vinosity as well as its perfect balance, this Tavel can be drunk as an aperitive. It would be best, however, to drink it with the slightly spicy dishes of world cuisine such as chilli con carne or couscous which will go very well with it, or sea fish served plainly grilled.

Domaine Bel Ange
FROM ONE ROOT TO THE NEXT

Miguelanje Garcia

'I took over the plot owned by my wife and having been making Tavel here since 1998. Before that, I was a farm worker. For a few years, I bottled my wine but since I own another business – earth-moving – I stopped bottling and I sell my wine in bulk. Ever since I became organic I've been thinking about switching back to bottling.

I have a very small plot of only four hectares, one hectare in Lirac and three in Tavel, on Les Vestides. The land does not yield much but the wines I made from it are of excellent quality. Since the estate has never brought in much money, I worked the land organically almost from the start, I always ploughed and finally I just had to fill in some paperwork without even having to change my ways, so that by 2012 I shall have the label.

I believe that in future there will be no other way of making Tavel except organically. It just needs a little more supervision and manual labour. Apart from that, I believe that working organically actually ends up costing less, at least for a small spread like mine. All I use now is copper, sulphur and elbow grease.

Now then, in my case, I don't need to earn a living from my vineyard, I live from my other occupation. So the grapes are secondary but I don't intend to get rid of them. They were inherited from my father-in-law who is no longer with us. We were very fond of him and he gave them to me, so I am their guardian. I'm a week-end wine-maker, but I enjoy it, I've been working in vineyards since I was fifteen. I prefer wines made in the traditional way, from grapes harvested by hand, something I can afford to do thanks to the size of my vineyard. For a large land-owner it would of course be harder to work in the way I do.

On my land, we all harvest together, we have lunch together in the vineyard, we drink an aperitive together, it's fun, it's tradition. People who harvest with me want to come back again. Not because they are paid to do so but so they can spend an enjoyable day. My parents are of Spanish origin, but I was born in Tavel, all my roots are here. I am a Tavel native and proud to be one'.

He plays the Flamenco guitar and loves to take a siesta. But you will have understood, he is a 100% Tavel native. Miguelanje is a tireless worker who tends his vines at the week-end and in the evenings. He is familiar with the tractor as well as with the good wine of Tavel. We can only hope that in a few months or years and perhaps at the very moment you read these lines, his Tavel will once again be available in bottles. Tavel will thus have an additional facet, a character trait, an additional style.

Domaine Bel Ange
Rue des Lauzes
30126 Tavel
Tel.: +33 (0)4 66 50 10 48
E-mail: michelsylvie93@hotmail.fr

Domaine des Carabiniers
AN ULTRA-DYNAMIC FAMILY

Christian and Fabien Leperchois

'My great-grandfather immigrated from Italy in the 1920s and set up a home on part of this property which became the basis for it. What does the name? Very simple. Pope Clement V had his summer residence at Roquemaure, and the road to Roquemaure was once guarded by a guard-post of riflemen (*carabiniers*).

Four nearly four decades now, I have had the good fortune and privilege of running this estate and developing it. Over the years, in the course of this exciting work, I have had an increasing urge to work more naturally, in fact, as our ancestors worked, to try and place the terroir in its natural surroundings. The only compromise that I have been able to find was converting to organic cultivation, which is indeed a reflection of respect for nature.

We try to offer the produce of the terroir, quality produce. It may not be better than the others but it has an identity that enables it to be known and recognised. I went organic in 1997. This was the period when we, the organic farmers, were considered a bit like the back-to-nature people of 1968, it was easy to make fun of us. For me, it was actually a more modern way of doing things. Technology enabled us to work under the best conditions to obtain the best products.

In 1997, we had to deal with our neighbours gently laughing at us, but I took it in good humour. Thirteen years later, many of our colleagues are moving in the same direction and in that way they are acknowledging that I was working for a better future.

We have witnessed a positive trend from conventional to organic farming. We wanted to push it even further and have chosen to move into biodynamic cultivation, a practice that makes us able to work towards sustainable agriculture, in greater harmony with the land and the cosmos. We basically use only two products, cow horn dung and silica, which we apply after one-hour's dynamisation.

We discussed it at length, we learned all about it, we tinkered with it in 2010, we continued in 2011, and the result was encouraging. Yet again, people think of us as being cranks, but the effect is so beneficial for the plants. I think that this is the near future for everyone.

By following the precepts of biodynamics, we can take more time to observe how growth develops, and to watch nature and the microfauna in the soil. We feel the beneficial effect on the wine which seems to be more mineral, more intense, even closer to the terroir'.

The result of their efforts can be found in the bottle. Their Tavel has a superb nose, with mineral, finely spiced notes of cinnamon and iron oxide, possessing structure and body. Christian, the father, and Fabien, the son, have achieved at least one of their aims, namely to create a Tavel wine of the highest class in the most natural way possible. Thanks to its robust, slightly peppery finale, its vinosity and perfectly controlled high alcohol content, it can be kept in a wine-cellar for several years and it suitable for accompanying at any time a grilled meat dish, sea fish or simply a delicious potato salad.

Domaine des Carabiniers
Tras le Puy
30150 Roquemaure
Tel.: +33 (0)4 66 82 62 94
E-mail: carabinier@wanadoo.fr
Website: www.carabiniers-vin-biologique.fr

Domaine Corne Loup
An almost feminine lightness

Géraldine Saunier

'My father, Jacques Lafond, left the cooperative cellar in 1966 to create his own estate from three hectares in Tavel. His cellar expanded in four stages, as the vineyard was enlarged, and I learned the job at his side. After working together for twenty years, he handed over management of the property to me. Being a wine-maker is a man's job and I find that women have difficulty making themselves felt, but here in Tavel, the cooperation is good, and more and more of us women are carrying on the good work.

Today, the estate covers 27 hectares in Tavel, but we also make Lirac and Côtes-du-Rhône red and white wines.

I love working with white wines, they did much to help me develop the vinification of my rosés. I am gradually trying to refine their style, I like lively, fruity Tavel wines, that may be powerful but that are easily drinkable. I am not too fond of heavy wines that are high in alcohol.

Vinification is the time I enjoy the most. It is an opportunity for experimentation and creativity and lets one move out of the ordinary. Naturally, this does not mean changing the typical features of Tavel wines. But thanks to the development of techniques such as settling, my wines have gained stability, their fruity expression persists for much longer.

In the vineyard, I have set myself the aim of gaining access to organic labelling in the next ten years. Currently, having to manage our 45 hectares all on my own, it is a little hard to switch, but I will get there.

I advise my customers to buy a little less but to come back every year. If we are going to benefit from its fruity character, my Tavel should preferably be drunk in the same year. It is the ideal wine for people who do not like mixing white and red, who want a single bottle that can be drunk throughout the meal'.

Touchingly sincere and defending work well done, all that this talented wine-maker lacks is – a little self-confidence! Her Tavel, after all, is one of the best of the cru. Fruity, drinkable, even delicate, with the tender feminine touch, it nevertheless possesses structure and thus typicality. We like it young and served a little colder as an aperitive or at just the right temperature with a crunchy seafood salad.

Domaine Corne Loup
Rue Mireille
30126 Tavel
Tel.: +33 (0) 466 50 34.37
E-mail: corne-loup@wanadoo.fr

Château Correnson
PASSION, FROM FATHER TO SON

Marc and Vincent Peyre

'We work together on a family property created in the 1980s. Prior to this, the farm grew grain, raised animals and there was some market-gardening. It emerged that we had good land for vines, suitable for producing quality wines. Our vegetables were average, but our wines are famous throughout the world. We therefore gradually abandoned mixed farming to devote ourselves entirely to wine-making. We offer generic Côtes-du-Rhône, Lirac in the three colours and, of course, Tavel. Producing wine is an exciting experience. Planting and tending to vines, wine-making, tasting, being in contact with the customers, expanding the property and now having to deal with exporting is an unusual adventure. Having a few plots of vines in Tavel was an old dream that finally came true with the new generation.

We were able to acquire four hectares from an estate that wanted to sell. It consisted of several plots situated on all the terroirs of Tavel.

Tavel is an exceptional cru which needs to be treated and vinified differently. We were making rosé in Lirac, but we needed to perfect our technique for making Tavel. What has changed the most is the way we have to tend the vines. Tavel soil is difficult to work, we needed more powerful tractors, more robust equipment. We equipped ourselves with pneumatic presses and a state-of-the-art refrigeration unit. We had to learn maceration something that is not usually the custom for Lirac.

We make rather traditional Tavel wines, very brightly coloured, powerful, that are full of flavour. This type of Tavel sells very well. It is an advantage to have Tavel, here in the vault as well as for export. Of course, people initially visit us to find a Château Correnson, but I think that Tavel is a sort of promotional product that helps to sell Lirac or Côtes-du-Rhône. In any case, quality wines will always sell, one just has to ensure they are top-of-the-range, that's all'.

I discovered this estate during my wanderings in the region and I immediately became a fan of their Tavel which is able to combine modernity with faithfulness to the style of the cru. It has a laudable clarity of expression, full of fruit and freshness, but it knows how to play the minerality card although it does not lack body. It is the very prototype of classic-contemporary Tavel which can be distinguished from the standard rosé by its deeper colour, more melting texture and aromatic richness. It can be drunk as an aperitive or tactfully and conservatively accompany dishes typical of southern France, such as fish baked in a salt crust, for example.

Château Correnson
Route de Roquemaure
30150 Saint-Geniès-de-Comolas
Tel.: +33 (0)4 66 50 05 28
E-mail: peyre-vincent@wanadoo.fr
Website: www.chateau-correnson.fr

Domaine de Lanzac
THE PLEASURE OF TYPICALITY

Lionel de Lanzac

'It all began in the 1950s. After the War, my grandfather, who was living in Avignon came to settle in Tavel. He bought a few hectares of vines, then he began to make his rosé and sell it direct, in bottles. At the time, a lot of bulk wines were being made. He decided to do something different and in order to be able to sell he would take it to the markets. That is why thirty years later, we continue to attend trade shows and fairs. My father Norbert took over the estate in the 1980s, and I have been working the vineyard for the past five or six years.

I believe that our Tavels are wines that are typical of the appellation. But above, all they are pleasure wines. By having attended so many markets and trade shows, we are very close to the customer, the consumer. Of course, we do some exporting, we sell to some of the major chains, but at a national level we tend to work mainly

Domaine de Lanzac
Route de Pujaut
30126 Tavel
Tel.: +33 (0)4 66 50 22 17
E-mail: domainedelanzac@hotmail.com
Website: www.domainedelanzacvindetavel.com

with individuals. We try to have a range – whether of our red wines or our Tavel wines – something for everyone. We vinify rosés that are suitable for all palates. We offer aperitive wines, wines for the summer, wines for the whole year, for Christmas dinner. We also produce Lirac and Côtes-du-Rhône, but in the case of rosé, we only vinify Tavel wine.

We produce three different types of Tavel. Our Grande Tradition, which I made in a very large volume, is the omnipurpose wine. I offer it in three vintages for a small clientele who like a slightly more aged Tavel. Of course, it is drunk differently. The range is supplemented by our two cuvees, Prestige and Plaisance, fruity, lighter wines each of which is only produced in two to three thousand bottles a year.

The Grande Tradition Cuvée is a typical Tavel wine, based on the three terroirs and most of the stocks used for the appellation. Our Prestige Cuvée is a pleasure wine par excellence and the Plaisance, cuvée is our summer wine. We put a little more Syrah in the Prestige and a little more Clairette in the Plaisance. As for vinification, I assemble all of the grapes from the various stocks and proceed to maceration. For making Prestige and Plaisance, I vinify Syrah and Clairette separately, then I blend them.

Like most of the people of Tavel, the Lanzacs, father and son, have understood that one needs to move with the times, while still keeping one foot in tradition. Their solution is to offer several cuvées. Their classic Tavel wine is one to be drunk with a meal, suitable for a little ageing, without frills, that one would choose to go with roast game or a rack of veal cooked with wild mushrooms.

Rosé, and thus Tavel, is often associated with summer. It is only chosen to eat with barbecued food even though it can be drunk year round. In France, a large Christmas feast is often prepared starting with a starter of fish or seafood accompanied by white wine, followed by red meat accompanied by red wine. A lot of my customers, however, do not like to mix wines and colours. For them, Tavel is excellent. They choose slightly older vintages that go particularly well with the occasion.

If I had more means and above all more time, I would try to experiment more. Not necessarily with the Tavel appellation. I might try vinifying in the cask, or offering sparkling wines, for example. I would have fun inventing, creating or developing other products, creating a brand name, why not?

The world of wine consumption has changed, people are drinking better and less. We are lucky became Tavel is a prestigious appellation making very nice products. We thus hope to be able to continue in this way, possible getting bigger, if possible. We work on about twenty hectares, eleven of which are in Tavel. That isn't a huge amount but it enables us to live and do what we like'.

Eric Grassone
AUTHENTICALLY NATURAL

Eric Grassone

'I was born at Villeneuve-Lès-Avignon, the neighbouring village to Tavel, and I have never left the region or my vines on the family estate. For more than twenty years I was a member of the cooperative but I dreamed of making my own wine. My first vintage dates to 2006, and I have the organic label since 2008.

I currently vinify two cuvées that I have decided to keep separately when it is time to blend them so that I can offer two types of Tavel wine, Li Bestiairi and Les Commeyres, creating through direct pressing and maceration like all the Tavels. The Li Bestiairi cuvée, produced from Grenache, Carignan and Cinsault stocks, is distinguished by its body and its structure, having a more masculine style. The Les Commeyres cuvée, vinified from the Grenache, Cinsault and Clairette varieties, expresses more lightness thanks to the latter white grape. It is thus not surprising that it is more pleasing to the palate of women who often perceive Tavel as wines as being too powerful.

My 5.5 hectares of vineyard cover two sites in which one finds three types of Tavel terroir. Blending takes place among the vines, I harvest in crates and once the grapes have been pressed the wine is made. I have not yet vinified plots separately up to now, I am only advancing step-by-step. I needed to explore this new wine-making venture because I have more experience in the vineyard. I learned wine-making late, as well as marketing.

My wines are not show animals, ready in March but undrinkable by September. They only express themselves fully after a few months of ageing.

I have no preconceived ideas about Tavel, I trust the consumer. The Tavel wine-lover claims to be more of a connoisseur than a mere drinker of rosé. He owns a cellar and he knows that he can keep a Tavel for several years and drink it at any time.

I chose to go for organic agriculture three years ago, and the organic processes extend to the cellar where I create my wines in a very craftsmanlike way. My aim is simple – to present unique wines created in a natural context so that they are appreciated for what they are, that is to say, authentic wines from start to finish'.

Eric built his house and his cellar with his own hands. From the roof of his home to the original architecture dominated by light and space, enjoying an exceptional view of Tavel and his vineyard. You reach the view by climbing a ladder, you need to make a little effort to be able to get up that high! But the sight is worth it! Do the same and make a little effort by storing the Li Bestiairi 12 cuvée, for up to 18 months in the cellar, decant it into a carafe and serve it with a dish of stuffed tomatoes, courgettes and peppers, and your taste-buds will also rise high! Or stay on t he ground and share a bottle of Commeyres as an aperitive, accompanied by bread spread with fresh goat's cheese.

Eric Grassone
Chemin des Comeyres
30126 Tavel
Tel.: +33 (0)4 66 50 25 24
E-mail: libestiairi@yahoo.fr

Domaine Fraissinet
A name that resonates

Monique Fraissinet

'When I was young, there were not so many vines in Tavel. There was mixed farming, the main crop was Tavel coco-beans, a variety that made the district during the war. In the morning, the men harvested the plants and in the afternoon the women and children sat in sheds, shelling and sorting the coco-beans. On one side there were those that were ready for selling and on the other, the dried and green beans, separated into different baskets.

After the war, the vine took over. The olive trees and cherry trees were grubbed up, nothing was grow except grapes. My parents did the same, they expanded, and today I own twenty hectares in Tavel that they left me.

I began working in the cellar at a very early age. My father and mother pressed the grapes with hand-presses on which I used

'He came and asked me all sorts of questions about how Tavel used to be, this Eric Pfifferling!' (read his portrait on pages 64-65), exclaims Monique Fraissinet. And yes, this octogenarian wine-maker remembers how Tavel used to be. Like Brother Roger de Manissy, she represents an inexhaustible source of information for those who want to know the history of the cru, for all the Tavel wine-makers who want to combine the present with the past.

But don't think she isn't thinking of the future. She very recently built one of the finest cellars in Tavel and is now considering starting to bottle! And so much for Marcel Guigal, the famous wine-merchant, her loyal customer for so many years who still visits her every year to stop at the Fraissinet cellar to choose Tavel personally!

to do gymnastics on the fixed bars. Of course, we had no swimming-pool or tennis courts so that on Thursdays, when there was no school we went to the vineyard with ploughs drawn by horses and enjoyed ourselves, my mother brought us a snack. Tractors arrived much later, in those days Tavel was much quieter. But I am not nostalgic for them, I live in my time.

I always ran the cellar, the workers and all that. My father died in 1980, and since I found myself all alone, I was forced to stop bottling. Since then, I sell to a Rhone merchant but with the economic downturn, a lot of merchants have disappeared or broken their contracts. Now the large groups are buying houses, close the local depots and thus rid themselves of the competition.

There is now only one merchant who regularly visits the cellar. His name is Mr Guigal d'Ampuis. He arrives with his son, they taste, they choose their wine. They are still true wine-merchants! I knew the father Guigal who would visit us with his son, now it is the turn of the son to visit us with his grandson. As for the rest, I don't see them any more, they send their cellar-master. Messrs Guigal d'Ampuis are the right type of people and it's always a field day when they visit.

In the past there were no œnologists. It was the merchant who gave us advice but, anyway, I took a course in œnology and I did the blending. Having workers in the cellar is not a good thing. I want to be in control, so I just get help with the rough work.

Tavel wine is made from grapes macerated for a whole night, then pressed. That is the way to make Tavel and in no other way. Tavel is not a *rosé de saignée*[1], it is a

VILLE D'AVIGNON

Foire de Printemps 1928

EXPOSITION DES VINS
du Vaucluse et des Côtes du Rhône

DIPLOME D'HONNEUR

décerné à Monsieur *Fraissinet-Taulier*

à *Tavel*

pour *son vin d'origine*

AVIGNON, le 6 Mai 1928.

Le Président.   Le Commissaire Général.   Le Maire.

wine somewhere between rosé and red, but since there is no name for this, it is called rosé. Tavel was always deep in colour. I have a document from Tavel's first wine-making syndicate that states: 'Tavel is not a rosé, it is a gold-tinted ruby wine'.

It isn't easy nowadays to run a vineyard like mine because the costs are enormous. Eight years ago we were still making money but today we barely get by. We have always known hard times, but they never lasted so long. Those who can manage are probably small land-owners who use a Moroccan worker who is paid the minimum wage. I think the future will be even harder. In the past, people worked to make Tavel famous. In those days, people lived modestly but now it's the new car, the television, the mobile phone…

The cooperative cellar has done a lot of good. Before that there were lots of small wine-makers who did not work very cleanly, the barrels were not property looked after. As soon as there was a wine-makers cellar, the quality of the wine changed, and the price rose immediately. My father was bottling in 1925 but he didn't want to join the cooperative. After his death, my mother wanted me to join it: 'You have too much work', she said to me. But well, I didn't want to. Perhaps today I would have decided otherwise. The cooperators have a slightly easier time of it. I need to be everywhere, I need to supervise everything. But I am continuing what I began and I don't regret it. I have built this new cellar – so I have everything I need – and I know the price of my wine. Despite everything, one can still live well in Tavel. Someone once said: 'Tavel is a name that resonates'. So we remain quite privileged.

1- Saignée, or bleeding the vats. The technique is used to give more tannin and color to a red wine, so some of the pink must is removed at an early stage. The red wine remaining in the vats is intensified as a result of this 'bleeding', because the volume of juice in the must is reduced, and the maceration is concentrated.

Domaine Fraissinet
Route de la commanderie
30126 Tavel
Tel.: +33 (0)4 66 50 06 88

Château la Genestière
A RATHER ORDINARY LIFE

Jean-Claude Garcin

'About 150 years ago, la Genestière was occupied by a silk thread-maker which used the water from the château's stream. In the 1930s, the property was converted to grape-growing, owning about forty hectares of vines at Tavel, about thirty at Lirac and thirty in the Côtes-du-Rhône. In 1994, we were able to acquire this magnificent estate, one of the most prestigious in the appellation.

My family comes from the Hautes-Alpes. My father was a milkman and I came to Tavel as an agricultural worker in the vineyards. In 1965, I began renting land and producing wine, while continuing to work for other land-owners. In 1969, I also started a market-gardening business, because at the time it was the only way for anyone with very limited means to earn a lot of money quickly.

In the early 1980s, I created from bare soil the first garden centre in the region. It did so well that in 1985, I decided to abandon market-gardening and devote all my time to horticulture. I grew early seedlings in Spain, created a nursery in Morocco where we grew small fruit-bearing citrus seedlings that we sent all over northern Europe – and so on. Wine-making had been a childhood dream of mine. I had an uncle who owned vines at Courthézon where I had worked during the school holidays since the age of six. That is where I caught the virus for this passion. That is why, from the beginning, I settled in Tavel where I was finally able to make my dream come true by buying this château where we live today.

What a life Jean-Claude Garcin has had! Or, rather, a number of lives! With all its ups and downs, he s till prefers to talk to us about his first obsession, his love and passion for hard work well done. This is a passion that his Tavel wines reveal at each sip. Thanks to their pleasant fruitiness and their balance, they are the perfect accompaniment to a pizza or a beef carpaccio laced with olive oil, a trickle of lemon juice and a few fresh basil leaves.

Having acquired the domain, we invested heavily in it as well as in the vineyard and the cellar which is equipped with the latest technology.

From our three types of terroirs in Tavel, we produce two different products, the so-called traditional cuvée, made from vines growing on lauses limestone on the Vestides, and the Raphaël cuvée made from grapes grown on the pebbly and sandy soil. It has a little more body than the traditional cuvée. This way, the customer has a choice. In any case, we sell both as well as each other.

We work in a very modern way. The harvest is chilled immediately it arrives in the cellar and is then transferred to the vats – which we call Elite vats – and we then proceed to a cold pre-fermenting maceration. We thus preserve all of the aromas of the fruit. We are making quite contemporary Tavel wines.

Today, my daughter works alongside me and runs the estate. My grandson, Eliott, is only thirteen, but obviously I hope that he will be inspired to carry on the good work!'

Château la Genestière
Chemin de Cravailleux
30126 Tavel
Tel.: +33 (0)4 66 50 07 03
E-mail: jc.garcin@domaine-genestiere.com
Website: www.domaine-genestiere.com

Domaine La Barrière
NOT AS SMALL AS ALL THAT!

Bénédicte and Philippe Brun

'In 1999, as a young farmer, I took over the family farm at Puyméras, in the Vaucluse, a few kilometres from Vaison-la-Romaine, where I created La Barrière estate. At the time, the property that had been purchased by my grandfather made Côtes-du-Rhône which was taken to the cooperative cellar.

In 1997, I married Bénédicte Amido of Tavel. When I settled here, I asked for and obtained the right to plant vines and after planting out my land at Puyméras, I still had some left over. So I asked my mother-in-law whether she had some virgin land in Tavel that she could give me. In 2003, I planted a vine on the lauses in the district of La Vaussière. That is how I became a grape-grower and wine-maker in Tavel.

This poor soil produced very fruity wines that were still well structured. In fact, it had already been planted with Grenache by my wife's grandfather. With less than one hectare in production, mine is certainly the smallest estate in Tavel that does its own bottling. We still have a way to go since we only had our first harvest in 2007. But I'm not unhappy with the quality we have obtained.

Tavel has opened the doors to the trade shows. They are overbooked with Côtes-du-Rhône, but there is less competition in Tavel wines. Having said this, the Tavel customer base is very special, it is not all that young and is gradually dying off. So we are trying to attract younger people, by producing Tavel that is a little paler in colour and above all more fruity.

It is not that easy at the moment. The fruitiness pleases the young people but the older ones prefer older wines. We try to do both, keeping as much fruit as possible at the start, without neglecting the structure and the keeping qualities.

Personally, I prefer Tavel that has spent two or three years in the bottle. Furthermore, I believe that Tavel cam never beat the competition from other rosés when it comes to freshness. That is why it needs to retain its typicality.

The people of Tavel have taught me a lot about vinification. At Puyméras, on the left bank of the Rhone, we do not have a strong wine-making history and my family has only been making wine for the past fifty years. Tavel is a place that has a long history of wine-making, the people of Tavel have had their private cellars for a very long time and their know-how goes back several generations.

At one time it used to be said: 'Well, we're not going to bring the horses back and start to plough again'. Yet now everyone, or almost everyone is digging out their old cultivators and rotivators. One cannot speak of respect for the soil and the terroir and continue to use chemical defoliants. We have taken the big step and we are in our third year of conversion to organic cultivation.

At the present time, many people are switching to organics, not out of conviction, but through commercial necessity, they are looking for a sales pitch. And why not, if it serves the environment? As far as I am concerned, it is not a mere consideration. On my grandparents' land we never used chemical defoliants, but we used systemic pesticides which I abandoned as soon as I took over the farm.

Organic farming? It just means working a little harder. But I'm not afraid of hard work. One might also accept a small reduction in yield and certain diseases might reappear but there is also a whole range of life that will come back into the vineyard.

For the moment, our aim is to be able to sell the 5,000 bottles of Tavel we make. Then we might drop in on mother-in-law to try and persuade her to let us have the heathland she still owns!'

We are certain he will make the best use of his mother-in-law's heathland. Philippe, a novice in Tavel, soon learned his lesson. True, the colour of his 2009, the wine he gave us to taste, is slightly paler than that of the classics of the appellation, but let us make no mistake. Behind this pale ruby robe there is a true Tavel in the mouth, powerful, fruity well-structure and full-bodied, so a wine to be drunk with a meal, to be chosen to accompany cassoulet, broad beans stewed with the local ham, a navarin of lamb, in short a cuisine full of flavour.

Domaine la Barrière
La Barrière
84110 Puyméras
Tel.: + 33 (0)6 17 06 70 72
E-mail: brunphilippe12@aliceadsl.fr
Website: http//domainelabarriere.fr

Domaine Lafond Roc-Épine
A NATURAL HERITAGE

Pascal Lafond

'Our 80 hectares covers four appellations – Tavel, Lirac, Châteauneuf-du-Pape and Côtes-du-Rhône. Our estate has belonged to the family for several generations and has its roots in Tavel. Four hundred thousand bottles, in good years and bad, are despatched from our modern cellar, which is lies on the road out of the village. Half of what we produce is Tavel wine. We have had certified sustainable culture for the past eight years, and been under organic conversion for the past two years, so the wines we produce are increasingly healthy, free of chemicals, environmentally- and consumer-friendly.

Organic cultivation is quite complicated but it's a sign of the times and there is a certain amount of media brain-washing about it. As far as we are concerned, it is the result of the discussions we have had about it for several years and over time it has become part of our natural heritage, having become indispensable to our way of cultivating and our convictions.

We have freed ourselves from the chemicals industry which long imposed on us products that were foreign to our living space. We did not know quite how to control them and the consumer was often afraid of them.

The change to organic growing had no effect on the quality of our wines. We have tried to work just as well as before but using different methods. Our aim is to create a Tavel that matches the changing tastes of the consumer from which one must never stray and know how to listen without losing our typicality that has made the appellation and the domain famous.

The consumer is more demanding and better informed than ever and seeks out quality to an increasing extent, creating a permanent stimulus in our search for the right product. The trend is for wines that are more supple, more complex, less dry and less vinous, wines with more body and more fruit.

I should like the property to remain in our family for a long time and for it to prosper by offering a wide range of quality product by combining tradition with continuity'.

The wine of this estate – fresh, easily drinkable, suave and supple, is one of the 'modernists' of Tavel, meaning wines with the flavour of today, free of nostalgia, vinified with care, but without repudiating its roots. Choose them as the perfect summer wines for a light barbecue, a family picnic or drink them at any time as an aperitive.

Domaine Lafond Roc-Épine
Route des Vignobles
30126 Tavel
Tel.: +33 (0)4 66 50 24 59
lafond@roc-epine.com
Website: www.roc-epine.com

Domaine Laurent
MARTINE AND THE GRAPE-GROWERS

Martine Laurent

'I inherited the family property from my mother in 2005. The estate has been in our family for several generations. I wanted to work with respect for tradition and the environment. That is why I opted for *Agriculture Raisonnée* [environmentally-friendly agriculture] certification. For a while, I vinified my Tavel on the premises of someone in the village, then the Roquemaure cellar asked me to do so, and since I was a member of this cellar that also vinifies my other grapes, it was perfectly natural for me to accept.

The Roquemaure cellar started in 1922 and has an exceptional working tool in the vats of the period combined with all the modern technology. Furthermore, it continues to be state-of-the art. The roof has been fitted with solar panels, we experiment with vinification without adding selected yeasts so as to be able to express the terroir and its specific characteristics more fully. I am therefore very proud of belonging to it and I think that for other wine-makers, it is a big advantage to be able to offer, along with Lirac and Côtes-du-Rhône, a cru as famous as that of Tavel.

Yves Pierlot, the cellar-master, vinifies the grapes I bring to the cellar. He also advises me on the right date to harvest from my three plots that are situated on two types of soil. He tastes the grapes and performs the necessary analysis. He then proceeds to macerate the grapes in the skin of the 40 or so hectolitres of Tavel that are harvested.

The Lirac rosé, also produced by the cellar, separately from the Côtes-du-Rhône and vins de pays, is closely related to Tavel, but does not possess its structure. The time taken for maceration at a low temperature in a drainage vat – 24 hours or more, depending on the harvest – is therefore longer for Tavel. Our wine, even though vinified outside the village, is one of the classics of the appellation, with a deep colour and a good structure.

For the past two years, all the wines in the Roquemaure cellar have been vinified without sulphiting prior to fermentation. To be able to do this, the grapes need to be in perfect condition. But sometimes you need to know how to take risks to be able to produce such an exceptional product!'

Exceptional – that is indeed Martine's wine – as well as that of Yves Pierlot and his colleagues who speak of it with equal excitement! The Roquemaure cellar thus has nothing to be ashamed of even though its Tavel is vinified 'abroad', some twenty minutes from the village. It is a deep ruby colour, with a very handsome spicy nose, redolent of berries and yellow flowers, with a nice mineral touch, and develops on the palate as juicy and fruity. It has all the qualities of a contemporary wine that is particularly well looked after that will please young people from the ages of twenty to one hundred and twenty. To be drunk without moderation on every occasion!
Rocca Maura –The wine-makers of Roquemaure

Cellier Saint-Valentin
1, rue des Vignerons
30150 Roquemaure
Tel.: +33 (0)4 66 82 82 01
E-mail: contact@vignerons-de-roquemaure.com
Website: www.vignerons-de-roquemaure.com

Domaine Maby
Wines that do not compromise

Richard Maby

'The Maby estate is one of the oldest in Tavel. We cultivate around 25 hectares there. We also produce Lirac wines, Côtes-du-Rhône and *vins de pays*. My family has been growing vines for two centuries, but their real occupation was that of shoemaker. At first the wine was destined for family consumption, vine-growing was just a hobby, then began to sell to the neighbours and gradually they started to distribute it throughout the region..

My grandfather became passionate about wine in the 1940s and decided that it would be his only occupation. He worked in the family vineyard and in the cellar, but to be able to make a living he needed to expand the property. He began to buy land so by the 1950s he had twenty hectares or so. The old cellar became too cramped so he bought the house we live in today and gradually around it he built all the cellar buildings which are now quite large and modern.

In the 1960s, he was joined by his children and he created the brand. He worked with his son, my father Roger, and his two sons-in-law, Christian Amido and Jacques Borelli, and both his brothers. The estate was then very large, consisting of around 120 hectares during the 1990s. At the time, it was certainly the largest estate in Tavel.

In the mid-1990s, my grandfather who must have been about 75 years old but who was still working, wanted to hand on the property. With their shares, my aunts created their own estates, the Amido estate and the Rocalière estate. My father kept the cellars of the Maby estate and a vineyard of about forty hectares. He continued to manage the property for about ten years while expanding it again. We currently farm about 65 hectares, and we have thus once again become a large Tavel estate.

I have always been interested in wine, but when I was younger, I couldn't really find my place on the property. Furthermore, I wanted to study, to discover the world, so for about fifteen years I worked on the Stock Exchange.

I took over the reins of the estate in 2005. It was the culmination of a passion and the start of an ambition. Wanted people to know that here in Tavel, as well as in Lirac, we had one of the finest terroirs in France. I am confident that we can produce extraordinary wines here, rosés with as much depth as the great red wines.

When I came back to the estate, I wanted to introduce a touch of modernity into our cultivation and vinification methods, and develop the aromatic potential of our wines. At every stage, from bringing in the harvest until vinification, we protect our wines from oxidation, but we do so naturally of course. And we work at very low temperatures during vinification, to extract the maximum of aromas. Our Tavel wines have remained rosés of maceration, concentrated rosés but with an improved aromatic expression.

Richard is not far from having succeeded in both his bets. As the fiery President of the Tavel appellation, he flies the flag for Tavel, travelling to distant lands, and in his capacity as a wine-maker he manages to combine tradition and modernity perfectly. Anyone wanting to learn how to recognise Tavel, you need to begin with the two products vinified with care and know-how, in which one presents as more elegant the other as being more powerful. You will understand the full scope of the possibilities of Tavel wines, and continue the discovery of other Tavel wines subsequently.

In the vineyard, we work in a very natural way. There are no insecticides, no weed-killer among the vines, no artificial fertiliser. We produce two cuvées, La Forcadière from the three terroirs in Tavel and thus very representative of the appellation, and Prima Donna, which comes exclusively from the round pebble soil.

Making a good wine is very simple, making a great wine is more complicated. Every detail needs to be meticulous. To make a great Tavel wine, you need a large grape, vinified with dexterity and uncompromisingly'.

Domaine Maby
249, rue Saint Vincent
B.P. 8
30126 Tavel
Tél. : +33 (0)4 66 50 03 40
E-mail : domaine-maby@wanadoo.fr
Site : www.domainemaby.fr

Domaine Le Malaven
History is never far away

Isabelle and
Dominique Roudil

'We settled here in 1999, and we created the Malaven estate on the basis of three hectares of Tavel, as well as one hectare of Lirac and a vin de pays from the family estate. We were then able to gradually expand the vineyard through purchasing and renting. Today, we own twenty-three hectares of which eight hectares are in Tavel. The buildings, the vault and the cellar were built in 2002.

Both of us come from Tavel wine-making families, so it is not surprising that we vinify a rather traditional Tavel. At the same time, we created a prestige cuvée produced from vines that are about forty years old planted on the sandy soil that produces a wine of a style that is more fruity and very fine but also powerful, qualities that are intrinsic for a wine to go with food. We are thus reviving the history of Tavel whose original vines were grown on the sandy soil. My father used to talk to us of the great finesse and elegance that are so special to this terroir.

Do not expect a modern, super-accurate, technological Tavel. Here, it is sincerity that takes precedence. Thus, Isabelle and Dominique offer two wines that are very much in their own image, classic, balanced, without frills that can be drunk throughout the year and that benefit from being decanted into a carafe. They go very well with pizza, fresh noodles with ham and with egg dishes, a pissaladière, and, possibly a crunchy Catalan coca baked in a wood-fired oven.

All of the main grape varieties are grown on the property, Grenache, Mourvèdre and Cinsault predominating of course. Cinsault was long denigrated for its high yield, but it makes a considerable contribution to the fruitiness and freshness of our wines. These three varieties are supplement by traditional Tavel stocks that give it its richness and diversity. If the Decree permitted, I would use more Cinsault since it still has a future.

Managing an estate that has only existed for ten years is becoming ever more complex in terms of the administration. It is hard to get into certain European markets where the laws are not the same for everyone. The most important constraints however are due to the climate, with bad weather and drought stress … Perhaps one day, we shall be allowed to irrigate, but that would not really be a solution because water might well become scarce very quickly.

I defend a vine that can be productive without additional help and that is most natural. I do everything that is humanly possible but for the rest I trust in nature. Fortunately, nature remains a factor that cannot be controlled'.

Domaine Le Malaven
Route de la Commanderie
30126 Tavel
Tel.: +33 (0)4 66 50 20 02
E-mail: dominique.roudil527@orange.fr
Website: www.domainelemalaven.com

Château de Manissy
In praise of slowness

Florian André

'The château dates from the sixteenth century and has changed owners several times. During the early twentieth century, it was occupied by missionaries of the Holy Family who are still the owners. They created the vineyard to provide wine for consumption within their community and wine for serving at masses for a large number of parishes.

The château has a collection of very old vintages. Our earliest Tavels date back to 1917, long before the area covered by the appellation was classified. Generations of wine-making monks succeeded each other until 2003, the year in which they put me in charge of managing the wine-making estate.

While the vinous and infinitely complex tête de cuvee is one of those rare wines that have no equal, the basic Manissy cuvée which is paler ruby with slight coppery reflections and delightful notes of broom, a touch of copper and fresh herbs is deliciously drinkable and smooth. It has an elegance that is almost outdated or rather, out of its time, and gains even more if aerated. There is something mystical about it, it is a wine for meditation par excellence. We tasted it while digesting several pages of the memoirs of Chateaubriand. Transcendent!

At the time, I was a very young grape-grower without much experience, even though my family has lived in Tavel for seven generations. My studies in Orange and Dijon and apprenticeships in Bordeaux enabled me to introduce new techniques and direct the estate towards organic cultivation and soon to be biodynamic.

Manissy own a unique terroir within the appellation, being situated at the edge of Tavel on terraces of sand and clay that ensure early maturing. What is special about the château is its vinification, illustrated by the *tête de cuvée*. To make this wine, I proceeded as in the olden days, to a slow fermentation in barrels, without filtration. The finished wine was only bottled one year after decanting from the basic vat. It is characterised by an incomparable authenticity. The idea of this pale red traditional wine of the type that was produced for centuries was developed by Brother Roger who spent thirty years working as a wine-maker in this estate. He patiently passed on to me his unique and valuable knowledge. s

Organic cultivation was the obvious thing to me. It suddenly clicked in 2009, when my son was born and I felt the need to protect us against all the synthetics. It has begun to motive all of the staff who immediately adopted the whole of this form of production, from the vine to the cellar'.

Château de Manissy
Route de Roquemaure
30126 Tavel
Tel.: +33 (0)4 66 82 86 94
E-mail: vins-de-tavel@chateau-de-manissy.com
Website: www.chateau-de-manissy.com

Mas Duclaux
A GOURMET PASSION

Benoît and
Nathalie Duclaux

'My wife Nathalie is the daughter of Henri Roudil and the granddaughter of Gabriel Roudil, two names that are well-known in Tavel wine-making. In this family, in which they have been wine-makers from father to son – and to daughter! – for five generations, I am a stranger, an interloper. I come from a long way away. I was born in Saint-Geniès, four kilometres from Tavel. Furthermore, I have never done this. My basic occupation is cooking.

We built the Mas Duclaux and took over twelve hectares of vines, five of them in Tavel, in 2006. The vines came from a family inheritance of Le Vieux Moulin estate. Since we decided to create our own brand, starting was not easy, the customers needed reassurance, but I think we have succeeded.

One does not become a wine-maker by accident, you need enthusiasm. It is a job that requires lots of time. Of course, having been a chef, I didn't have the necessary knowledge for wine-making, so at the start it was my father-in-law who taught me, then my nephew, Sébastien, who continued. They put their knowledge and experience at my disposal. I had my own ideas, my taste, I always considered wine as something to go with food. Nathalie and I have strong characters and our Tavel is like us.

We produce wines for gastronomy. For wine to accompany food, it needs to be powerful, with body and structure that has something to say to you. If you prepare a dish, it needs to tell you a story, it needs to be appetising. In our Tavel, the colour also counts.

Naturally there are foundations to be respected in this appellation. You don't invent something new from one day to the next. It remains immutable like a tree trunk, but there are branches that grow, leaves that change. In any case, it is the consumer who decides whether he likes our wines and if he does he will come back. A small estate like ours needs to find a niche market with products that are something of a luxury, we are too small to be able to tackle the large export markets.

One day, perhaps, I can bring my two passions, food and wine, together. Why not invite guests and show them this happy marriage? I should love to serve our wines accompanied by a slightly spicy cuisine, maybe oriental cuisine or with French cuisine, choosing roast game, dishes normally served with red wines but which go extremely well with our dense and well structured Tavels'.

This Tavel is a dark rosé with ruby reflections. It has an impressive aromatic cleanliness with notes of berries, flowers and spices, a dynamic, perfectly balanced structure, and thus all of the qualities sought in a light red wine. It will thus go well with all the dishes that require a fruity Tavel with a certain powerfulness. We would suggest it for creative, contemporary cuisine based on fresh produce of the finest quality. Taste it with home-made fresh ravioli, accompanied by stuffed yellow e courgettes served with cream and basil – and let us know how it tasted!

Le Mas Duclaux
Chemin de Vallinière
30126 Tavel
Tel.: +33 (0)4 66 50 10 61
E-mail: nathalie.duclaux@wanadoo.fr
Website: www.caveroudilduclaux.fr

Maison Méjan-Taulier

A VERY SPECIAL CELLAR

Florence Méjan

'My grandfather, Valéry Taulier, created our House in 1920, so I represent the third generation of the family. Originally there was a little cellar in the village, but then he moved it to here.

At the time, it was the only cellar in Tavel owned by an individual. My grandfather, who was a wine-maker, merchant and exporter, travelled a lot in Switzerland and Germany, then later, his son-in-law, André Méjan, my father, perpetuated the family tradition.

I took over in 2007. I have always known the property, I was born here, so it was perfectly natural. We children took part in the summer activities. There was no labeller, all labelling was done by hand. Visitors were very impressed by the cellar, for me it was just part of the furniture.

Today, I mainly deal with marketing the wines and the administration of the estate. In only visit the cellar from to time to give them a hand, because I'm short of time. I regularly taste our wines, I even drink them and I do so with great pleasure!

Our wine is the faithful reflection of our terroir, as well as the spirit of this traditional House. The grapes we use in our Tavel, which is known as Canto Perdrix, come almost exclusively from the round pebbles terroir. The base is 80% Grenache so this is a wine that is full of character. That is how it should be. The wine is the fruit of its terroir, but there is always something in it of the character of the wine-maker.

We have something extraordinary to work with here, so we could always go further as far as quality is concerned. We have made a lot of progress since 2007, and I'm sure we'll be able to do even better'.

With the assistance of Charles-Richard Farago, Florence Méjan bears a heavy responsibility, that of managing the first private cellar founded in Tavel. Ever since she took over the House, her Canto Perdrix, a classic, well-made Tavel has been granted awards several times. It goes very well with roast pork, prunes and black mushrooms, or any other type of white meat served in its own cooking juices.

Maison Méjan-Taulier
Canto Perdrix
Place Président Leroy
30126 Tavel
Tel.: +33 (0)4 66 50 04 02
E-mail: domaine.mejan@orange.fr
Website: http//mejan-taulier.com

Prieuré de Montézargues

THE CHALLENGER OF ROSÉ

Guillaume Dugas

'This twelfth-century property is the last Tavel estate, determining the eastern and southern boundaries of the appellation. In the Middle Ages, Montézargues Priory belonged to the monks of the Grammont Order. Wine has been made here for at least eight hundred years. At first, production was destined solely for consumption by the friars. After they left in the thirteenth century, the prior changed hands several times, but all the owners devoted themselves to wine-making. In 2003, the Richard family of Paris, well known coffee-roasters, purchased the estate and asked me to manage it. I am a native of Vaucluse, and before coming here I had only made red wines., but I was very keen to make rosés. It was a real challenge and has remained so until this day.

At Montézargues, we have sandy soil that produces very fine rosés and Grenache does very well here. We work our wines a little like white wines with fairly short maceration to prevent the colour darkening, and we allow our wines to settle. We then decant part of the chilled grape juice and recover it later. That is where we recover the primary aromas of the fruit, that are so important for us.

The Tavels I enjoy today are balanced wines, that are fruity but that have good keeping qualities. They can withstand seven or eight years ageing in the bottle, even longer. I love to produce wines that present with a certain acidity and thus with freshness and longevity.

What about the future? Of course, it's unfortunate not being able to make red wines in Tavel, because we also own extensive red wine lands here, but we are restricted to producing great rosés. And that may even be a good thing. This way, we can allow wonderful rosés to develop of which I shall certainly never grow tired'.

One could accuse the Guillaume, the talented wine-maker of having too modern an approach. The wine is lighter in colour and it has notes of nectarine and citrus in the nose, which at first approach are similar to those of a white wine. But what follows in the mouth is 100% Tavel. We discover body, structure and length, even a certain amount of power, and all this in a style that is perfectly controlled, precise and balanced. It should be drunk cold as an aperitive or with a seafood salad.

Prieuré de Montézargues
Montézargues
30126 Tavel
Tel.: +33 (0)4 66 50 04 48
E-mail: gdugas@prieuredemontezargues.fr
Website: www.prieuredemontezargues.fr

Domaine de la Mordorée
A DISTINCTIVE TAVEL

Fabrice and Christophe Delorme

'Our estate was created in 1986. Although I was actually trained in viticulture, I come from wine-making stock. Our family has been producing wine since the sixteenth century. After trying biodynamics, the estate very much favoured organic cultivation. In 2010, we took the plunge and started to convert our land with the aim of being organically certified in 2013. All of the 54 hectares were converted to organic, the 26 hectares in Lirac, the 11 hectares in Côtes-du-Rhône, the 9 hectares in Tavel, the 5 hectares in Châteauneuf-du-Pape and the 3 hectares of *vin de France*.

One of the fundamental aspects of our work is to ensure the good health of our soils. Our ancestors bequeathed our terroir to us, and we want to be able to do the same, in all its fecundity, for our children.

Grapes are harvested manually and sorted on the vine. We have no second wine. Another fundamental aspect of our philosophy, apart for respect for the terroir and nature, is respect for people and thus for our customers. One of our main goals has been to create the finest possible expression of each of the AOC wines we produce. With this in mind, we asked a well-known specialist to make a thorough study of our terroirs which would now enable us to work even more accurately, providing each soil type with exactly what it needs.

Since we are both gastronomes and inveterate gourmets, we have created a large number of recipes with chefs and cordons-bleu cooks so as to develop food that goes best with our wines, which are real wines for the table.

Our Tavel wines express fruitiness, a wonderful pale ruby colour, persistence in the mouth and complexity. They have sufficient body to accompany the finest dishes, good keeping qualities of an average or six years, ten years or more for the great vintages. Since 1986, we have won an impressive number of medals and distinctions. Thus, in 2009, Robert Parker awarded our Tavel wine the highest mark every received by a dry rosé. This may explain why we export 35% of our production of Tavel to twenty-three different countries'.

For nearly two decades, they were my only contact with Tavel, and their fruity, juicy wines, worked very precisely, remain unbeatable. Francis, the communicator and Christophe, the vine-grower, the man of the soil, have even crossed an additional frontier. Their two Tavel wines have gained in depth and in soul, and few foods can resist them. A lobster salad, an omelette with ceps, grilled pork, a Moroccan tagine or Cantonese-style chicken with bamboo shoots are just a few examples of a cuisine without borders for wine without limitations.

Domaine de la Mordorée
Chemin des Oliviers
30126 Tavel
Tel.: +33 (0)4 66 50 00 75
Email: info@domaine-mordoree.com
Website: www.domaine-mordoree.com

Domaine Moulin La Viguerie
THE SCIENCE OF SENSITIVITY

Gaël Petit

'I was born in 1970, exactly one hundred years after my great-grandfather who was president of the appellation and responsible for the documentation when it was first classified. Our wine-making roots date back to the sixteenth century.

The first Roudil in the village was recorded in the 1560s, and he was listed as the owner of a vineyard, grape-growing was his main activity. Even though we possess other documents witnessing the wine-making activity of our family at various eras, we lack the complete sources to trace our family accurately.

The story of our estate is similar to that of many others in the Tavel appellation. In the course of generations, family properties were split up, reconstituted, recreated, redistributed destroyed or reconstructed. Originally, there was a system of alliances through endogamy, marriages took place within the village, which made it possible to keep inheritance relatively intact and concentrated. For the past generation or two, the configuration has changed, people marry outside and so there is a lot of movement of plots of land from generation to generation.

Just like my grandfather who reconstituted his estate after it had been split several times, I am in the process of reconstituting mine when the estate of my grandfather, Gabriel Roudil, disappeared in1998. Depending on the generations, taking over and running a property like mine is fairly easy. As long as it is split up only between parents and children, the concept of brotherly affection is still present, and there is a strong bond of unity.

The specific nature of the estate is linked to my personality. I was brought up with my grandparents and my grandfather, a man of strong personality who was very upright, made a strong impression on me. He would take me with him into the vineyard and he taught me to taste wine.

Even in those days, I was in direct contact with the vine and with wine. I remember us as a very happy family. We would play among the tractors with our cousins, but when it came to the succession, relations became slightly strained.

In my political science studies, I tackled the subject of rootedness and human collectivity. This subject has strongly influenced my approach to wine. I have been familiar with the technique since childhood, but techniques such as inhibiting malolactic fermentation or the decision to let it proceed are only methods from which one needs to emancipate oneself. Wine affects the essence of the wine-maker's personality, his state of mind. For me, it is a passion. My ethic can be summarised in three concepts: the land, the objective element, willpower, the wine-maker's decision and humility, the limitations imposed by our finiteness.

Gaël seems to oscillate permanently between the exact science he has learned and his intuition, sensitivity, experience of life, and feelings that of which he has such as abundance. The same applies to his wine. It has an exemplary rigour and technical expertise, with its superbly fresh mouth, density, vinosity and with a depth aromatic complexity that are rare, its notes of rose-hip, pink grapefruit and toasted almonds, it is also gifted with an evident sensuality. Reserve it for matching with choice dishes, a lobster salad on a bed of pink grapefruit or the finest farmhouse cheeses, the best Pyrenean lamb, the most perfect goat's cheese from the Loire, or a true Swiss Emmental that has been well-aged in a cellar.

Wine is cyclic. It is born and disappears and thus is an invitation to detachment. The enthusiasm and freedom of the wine-maker are concepts that I would love to share with the consumer. My Tavel is linked to an art of living, a sort of inebriation in the noble sense of the word, in an intellectual and spiritual balance that brings joy, sensuality and contemplation'.

Domaine Moulin La Viguerie
104, rue de la Combe
30126 Tavel
Tel.: +33 (0) 466 50 06 55
E-mail: gael.petit2@wanadoo.fr

Domaine des Muretins
WORDS OF WINE

Benoît Roudil

'Our estate currently consists of twelve hectares. The cellar was built by my grand-father in 1966 and enlarged as the area under cultivation expanded. Seven hectares are within the Tavel appellation and five hectares are in Côtes-du-Rhône. We are a true family enterprise in which everyone lends a hand. The vineyard, which is representative of the various Tavel terroirs, covers the *lause* limestone, pebbles, sand and a mixture of limestone and clay, on which almost all the stocks of the appellation are grown. The age of the vines varies between 40 and 65 years. I only vinify a single Tavel. I defend my freedom and do not belong to any school, I remain faithful to the way my parents made wine and enrich myself from the experience of competent people.

'I do not know how to talk about my wines, my wines have to do the talking for me', he says with sincerity. So let them have their say, let us drink their words, inhale their fruity notes of strawberries and raspberries, delight in the tenderness, suppleness and balance that they have in such abundance. Keep them for drinking as an aperitive, enhanced by a few carefully chosen tapas or a fresh, summer menu.

We never harvest a whole vine during the day, we gather by vine stock, plot by plot. We try to blend immediately after harvesting and depending on the expression of the aromas, and we eventually rectify the drawing-off after fermentation. The aim is to reveal the complexity and characteristics of the varieties. We pay special attention to the delicate bouquet of Clairette that is used in almost 25% of our blends.

Our colours are fairly deep. We produce wines for the table. I like to associate my wines with sea fish, they go amazingly well with grilled bream on a bed of wild fennel, or with sea-bass – but it will even work well with pizza or with white meat. And of course I serve it as an aperitive.

I sell a great deal of my wines directly, the rest are marketed by the trade. The future of estates such as ours tends to be organic. I started converting it this year. It's not all that difficult to set up. You just need to spend more time in the vineyard, work a little harder as well, but it's for our future. What is my dream? It came true this year! I was finally able to afford the press I needed to be able to work they way I want! My other dream would be to be able to increase the number of hectares so I could live better, be more visible and, of course, expand the cellar. But sales of land in Tavel have become rare'.

Domaine des Muretins
19 chemin de Vacquières
Chemin de Vallinière
30126 Tavel
Tel.: +33 (0)4 66 50 36 12
E-mail: domainedesmuretins@orange.fr

Palai Mignon
Instinct first

Cyril Amido

'I spent fifteen years as a member of the Tavel Cellar cooperative. In 2005, to branch out on my own, built a cellar and vinify my first vintage. From being a grape grower I suddenly turned into a wine-maker but I did not forget my original calling.

I also pay the greatest attention to the quality of the grape. What happens afterwards in the cellar is much less decisive. There is little to distinguish between the vinification of one Tavel and another. In fact, all it needs is to be attentive. There may well be some differences between one estate to the next, but they are minimal. But the same is not true with respect to one grape and the next.

The choice of leaving the Tavel cellar was one of logical progression. The wine I vinify myself is the culmination of my work throughout the year. In the past, the result of my efforts was lost in the mass, today it is palpable, it's in my bottle.

The vineyard has been organic since 2011. To stay as close as possible to nature and stay faithful to the expression of a vintage, I intervene as little as possible in the development of the grape and its transformation into wine. But beware! Organic cultivation is not a synonym for letting things go to pot. I'm not good at the scientific and chemistry side personally, and that's why I prefer to rely on my instinct. That is what determines from one day to the next whether my vineyard needs targeted intervention or not.

Organic cultivation is more in harmony with nature than farming that uses chemicals. We are more on the alert. The two basic products I use are copper and sulphur.

My style? I don't know if I have a style. I only seek to best transmit the concept of terroir and the vintage. To respect each of them, since each of them has an important on the taste of the wine that can thus be slightly altered.

Continuing to work in this way signifies defending craftsmanship, as far as I am concerned, it is more conscientious, more controlled as well as more human, in contrast to the eternal race for profitability by a society in which everything is prefabricated and reheated, and in which one has to move faster and faster'.

Cyril is able to do just about anything. And to do it well! This man of the vine and former member of the cooperative has been very successful in transforming himself into a wine-maker and the ambassador for his cru. If he isn't sitting on his tractor or working in his cellar, he advises his passing customer in his pretty little vault in the centre of the village. We tasted his 2009 – proof of how well it keeps, Cyril's Tavel. Supple, but nevertheless well structured and full of vigour, with lovely notes of development. We chose it– and chose well – to go with a cheese plate.

Palai Mignon
Le Palai Nord
Route de la Commanderie
30126 Tavel
Tel.: +33 (0)4 66 82 89 26
E-mail: cyril.amido@orange.fr

Domaine Pélaquié
MATURITY AND BALANCE

Luc Pélaquié

'I run a large 80-hectare family estate. We mainly produce Côtes-du-Rhône and Côtes-du-Rhône Villages Laudun and Lirac wines, as well as a little Tavel. Tavel only represents 3% of our harvest. It is certainly easier to sell Tavel since it is very well-known.

Regardless of the appellation, our approach to grape-growing is the same. We need to bring healthy, ripe grapes to the cellar. We have the advantage of having a lot of sun where we are and the wine needs to be the reflection of this generosity. Because our Tavel has a spicier structure than a light rosé, it is more suitable as a wine to have with food than an aperitive wine. It comes from the limestone *lauses* that give it depth. For greater smoothness, we harvest the grapes when they are fully mature. Naturally, the alcohol is high. Of the three grape varieties we use, perhaps we should use more of the Cinsault. An estate of this size constantly needs to be questioning itself when it comes to marketing – something for which we are entirely in charge – as well as production, to adapt to current tastes.

Soon, the greatest problem our terroirs will face is lack of water. One can only obtain great wines of superb maturity if the plant possesses a certain balance. If nature does not do more to help us, increasing production, working in a good cellar and creating wonderful wines will be impossible. To avoid irrigation, we ought perhaps to be considering areas once considered too damp'.

Just as we were leaving his estate, Luc Pélaquié gently placed in our hands, apart from his Tavel, a bottle of his Laudun blanc. This confirmed his mastery of vinification. This know-how has also benefited his Tavel, with its dense, well structured, vinous intensity and remarkable length. It should preferably be served in a carafe, in order to release its finely spiced notes, accompanied by lamb cutlets grilled with herbs.

Domaine Pélaquié
7 rue Vernet
30290 St Victor La Coste
Tel.: +33 (0)4 66 50 06 04
E-mail: contact@domaine-pelaquie.com
Website: www.domaine-pelaquie.com

Domaine Roc de l'Olivet
NATURE DOES NOT WAIT

Thierry Valente

'One day, my father gave me a bottle of Roc de l'Olivet 1937. Then, at the very time that the Tavel cellar was being created, the estate disappeared. Wine-makers formed different groups to make their wine and extract a better living from it. In 1996, the estate was split and bequeathed to the four children. I took over my share and with it the name, but on one condition – I wanted to leave the communal cellar and produce my own wine.

I learned wine-making on the job. Of course, I adopted certain techniques such as chilling, everyone does that, but apart from that, I make wine in my own way. I appear to be successful, my wine is not unknown – but I'm not quite sure why. It must be due to a host of small details, but honestly I don't see what I'm doing that's so special.

As for the vineyard, it's very small. I began with two hectares. Today, I have five hectares of which four are productive. What do I do there? I watch the grapes and as soon as they are ripe, I pick them, I don't wait. I pick them on the vine, I want them to retain their notes of red berries. We harvest in the morning, after a hearty breakfast, then we stop when lunch is ready. We don't harvest in the afternoon.

I have plots on all the types of terroir, in the plain, in the Vestides, on the slopes and at the foot of Vallongue. I like the suppleness of the wines of the plain, their lightness complements the more structured wines of the slopes so well.

I adore my job – growing the vines as well as working in the cellar. But sometimes, both of them get on my nerves. When I clean out the cellar, I prepare everything to be ready just before the harvest and that's the most difficult time. Afterwards, the atmosphere in the cellar returns to normal, the grape juice, the odour of the must, all that, and I feel good. It's like a drug.

In the vineyard, working the soil, tracing the development of each plot, I'm constantly on the move. Nature advances and you run after it. And then, the grapes are maturing increasingly fast. Well, you get there in the end. By working with nature, we really understand the concept of passing time, the seasons and all that. Nature does not wait for you, if you let it get away from you, you will never catch up with it.

I hope that my grandson will take over the estate but he's only three years old so I need to wait for a while. But I'm happy with what I do, I sell the wine I love, and that's not such a bad thing. As long as I enjoy it, I'll continue to do so'.

After this, when I tasted it, I understood why his wine is so good. Because it's like him. It has finesse, kindness, modesty, balance, elegance and depth, as well as this love of careful work – everything is there in the bottle – and there is nothing to be bashful about! I would choose Thierry's wine for what it is. Without an accompaniment, in a moment of happiness and tranquillity. With a good book, perhaps. Or sharing it with someone I love.

Domaine Roc de l'Olivet
Chemin de la Vaussière
30126 Tavel
Tel.: +33 (0)4 66 50 37 87
E-mail: valente.thierry@wanadoo.fr

Domaine Saint Ferréol
RESPECT THE VINE

Jean-Marie Bastide

'I started working with my grandfather in 1977. My great-uncle died in 1983, and I had the possibility of taking over part of his property. His name was Ferréol and he lived in the rue Saint-Ferréol – Saint-Ferréol is the patron saint of the village, so the name for the estate I have been running for nearly thirty years came ready-made. The vines on the property are only old ones that I work in the same way that my grandfather did. I am against chemicals but I do not cultivate organically. I think that what they now call "organic" is not truly organic. Most of the organic growers do so purely to ensure their land is more profitable, they are not true believers. To really go organic means working the land with a mule and getting rid of the harvesting machine that consumes 120 litres of diesel a day. Really farming organically is something you need to do from start to finish, it's a mentality. There's a rush to turn organic now in Tavel, but it's not from true belief. There are a few rare individuals who genuinely do it out of conviction and these people do not even write it on their bottles. Above all, you need to respect the vine, and it will respect you back. It gives what one gives it. If it's given chemicals, it will give back chemicals. Forcing the yields, is like growing grapes without soil. The maximum you can get is 35 hectolitres per hectare. And you need to work pretty hard to achieve that naturally. Getting more than that is madness. In the first decree for the appellation which was created by my great-grandfather and Baron Leroy, the limit was 37 hectolitres. They chose this because no one had ever achieved it and, after them, no one will ever do so either. That way, they made everyone happy. But nowadays, with artificial fertiliser once could easily exceed it. Diluting the wine in that way, it would no longer be like anything and it would certainly not be a Tavel. I work my land and I have noticed – in fact, that is what it appears to me, but it concerns no one but me – that they are suffering slightly less from the drought we have been experiencing for several years. I try to make wines that are like those that were made in the past, but naturally using recent techniques such as chilling which enables us to extract more aromas. The wines that are like the wines that made Tavel successful, that are quite dark in colour, cannot be made every year. In any case, as far as I am concerned, a Tavel rosé does not resemble the typical rosé. The colour is deeper, structured, dense, Tavel is a wine that has keeping qualities. Today, unlike what some people seem to think, we cannot recover the commercial advantage that was stolen from us by other appellations that have made rosé so successful, by making marketing a priority, with a paler, lighter wine. If we did, we would be drowned by the masses. I'm not worried for myself. I have a small estate, my customers are loyal and range from the elderly to young people, and the restaurateurs I supply have trusted me for many years. What is my dream? My grandfather made Tavel the leading rosé appellation in France. I should like us to become the first truly organic appellation in France, that all the chemicals, weed-killers and fertilisers be forbidden or at least a reasoned argument is made for such treatments, but weed-killers are no longer used. If people worked the soil and did more in their vineyards, they would soon see the difference, their wine would acquire value, not monetary value, but sentimental value'.

His frankness will have disconcerted quite a few people. But Jean-Marie Bastide is right because it is only with heart and common sense that one gets things done. He does not shrink from the task of producing a Tavel that resembles a true wine, a deep red wine with a hint of floral and mineral notes, a superbly smooth mouth, juicy, fruity, long and rich, but without excessive alcohol. It is the best wine to serve with a meal, made for making friends that one can share around a good table, loaded with simple but succulent dishes, such as a good roast, a piece of meat from a true craftsman butcher who knows how to age his product and give good advice about it, or a freshly caught trout, or a fine Comté AOC cheese that has been aged for 24 months.

Domaine Saint Ferréol
Rue Frédéric Mistral
B P 15
30126 Tavel
Tel.: +33 (0)4 66 50 47 10
E-mail: jeanmariebastide@orange.fr

Château de Ségriès
Changing with the times

Henri de Lanzac and Frédéric Grasset

'I was born in Avignon. The Tavel property comes to us from my mother, my father was originally from the Auvergne. He came to Tavel, met my mother, and then *voilà*! When I had the opportunity to acquire a château with its cellar and a good piece of land in Lirac, I did not hesitate for a second and I left the village – without really leaving it – because we continue to produce Tavel wine. At present, it is much easier to sell Tavel than Lirac. But I think that the Lirac will make progress. Today, everyone asks us for a very fruity wine that can be drunk all year round. We therefore work with this in mind. In our Tavel, we are almost looking for the flavour of pear drops. So what we produce is quite modern, while hoping we are not mistaken, of course. We happen to believe that Tavel loses a little if one waits too long. Of course, it will keep for two or three years in the bottle, but it does not really improve much in quality. Of course, at one time, Tavel was only sold when it had aged for a year. It was the tradition. Ah! Tradition! One also needs to move with the times! So we are trying to make contemporary Tavel, but of a very high quality, containing a lot of fruit, as well as length, body and balance. Tavels for our time, I mean! Not a Tavel that makes too many concessions to fashion! The fashion is for pale rosés, ours retains its bronzed ruby colour. This having been said, each estate works in its own way. That's how it should be. We make the wine that we like and it sells quite well. Others make wines of a different style and as long as they sell well, there's no disadvantage in that. People are drinking less and less, but they becoming even more demanding as far as quality is concerned. If a wine-maker does not produce quality, he is quite simply a dead man. So we try and follow the technical development to gradually invest in equipment that is increasingly sophisticated. It all depends on our resources. Today's Tavel is not the same Tavel of ten years ago and who knows what tomorrow's Tavel will be like. There may be new varieties, more restrictions… The world moves so fast, one needs to know how to adapt to it. When you get up in the morning, you need to challenge yourself, automatically'.

Henri de Lanzac teaches wine-making wisdom to his son-in-law Frédéric Grasset, husband of his daughter Anne. But despite his reputation as a quality wine-maker, he does not hesitate to seek advice elsewhere. Consequently, for the vinification, he gets support from the œnologist Gérald Lafont. And the wine shows it. There is fruit, minerality and crunchiness as well as substance. This is a classic Tavel but in the spirit of the age, to be chosen as an aperitive or to go with a light and refreshing appetiser.

Château de Ségriès
Chemin de la grange
30126 Lirac
Tel.: +33 (0)4 66 50 22 97
E-mail: chateaudesegries@wanadoo.fr

Domaine des Six Deniers

A PEASANT AND PROUD TO BE ONE

Grégoire Michel

'I took responsibility for the paternal property in 2000. Our estate is in the commune of Saint-Marcel-de-Careiret, about thirty kilometres from Tavel, where we mainly make Côtes-du-Rhône. So I'm a foreigner! (*he smiles*). The Tavel plots are an inheritance from my mother's side, she was born in the village. They were incorporated into the family estate in 1996, but we were making their grapes into wine in my uncles' cellar until 2009. It is only since the 2010 vintage that we have been putting the grapes into vats in Saint-Marcel where I have now finished building my own cellar. So it's the start of a great adventure! Our 4.20 hectares of Tavel are on two types of land. At Vallongue, they grow on soil strewn with smooth pebbles combined with clay and sand and with a fully southern exposure and in the Plain, on sandy soils. To be able to vinify Tavel, a wine that is known throughout the world, is a big advantage for our operation, it almost certainly helps us a bit to sell our other wines. My first 'solo' vinifications of Tavel went very well. I was able to benefit from the advice of my family in the village who were happy to impart their knowledge to me. This will also help me with the vinification of the wines of other appellations. I like deep rosés. A true Tavel should be vinous, slightly spicy, but with a hint of mildness. It is made to be drunk at the table, with sweet-and-salty combinations of local or foreign dishes and goes wonderfully with Chinese cuisine. Despite the economic downturn, I am gradually continuing my expansion but at a measured pace. In any case, I don't have much choice. If you don't move forward you go backwards. I am a peasant and proud to be one, I feel very close to my land. It is the land that has taught me to walk before I can run'.

True, he doesn't live in Tavel, but his 2010, the first that Grégoire has been able to vinify with talent in his new cellar, is now one of the fundamentals of the appellation. It has a deep colour, possessing fruitiness, crunchiness and roundness. The mouth is rich and full, a true Tavel wine to be matched with food, to be served at table with stewed ceps or, better still, with duck with orange, since it does not balk at acidity, nor sweet and salty flavours.

Domaine des Six Deniers
30330 Saint-Marcel-de-Careiret
Tel.: +33 (0)4 66 33 59 04
E-mail: domainedessixdeniers@orange.fr

Domaine de Tourtouil
First let's talk of rosé

Christine Lefèvre

'In 1937, when the cellar of Tavel wine-makers was inaugurated, my grandfather was a founder member and thirty years later, he helped my parents build their own cellar on the Tourtouil estate. The name means 'a sinuous little stream'. I took over the estate about five years ago.

We only bottle a quarter of our production, the rest leaves in bulk. But I may be the last estate in the village to produce nothing but Tavel wine. It is not that easy to sell a single product, even if it is Tavel. In the past, people drank Tavel because we were practically the only ones in the region to produce quality rosés. Today, everyone offers quality wines in the three colours. Our success is therefore slightly old-fashioned. At the risk of shocking everyone, I would say that if I could change the decree, I would produce all three colours in Tavel. We have the terroirs for it! My vineyard, which is worked conventionally, but in an environmentally friendly way, is very disparate. I have plots in the three terroirs. I then blend them. So I only sell a single cuvée in bottles. I make my Tavel slightly paler than everyone else and it is very fruity, while remaining in the traditional style, with an added feminine touch. At the risk of displeasing some people, I believe that those who make ruby-coloured Tavel are mistaken in the message. The customers will then expect a red wine and that annoys me. I want to make true Tavel rosé. Working organically? I would be tempted if it didn't require such a lot of labour. Not everyone can allow themselves the luxury of employing more workers. In my opinion, the whole appellation should be organic, it would be more logical, and if this happened I wouldn't hesitate. It's not always easy to be respected as a woman, but I was born here, and I have always done this job, so it's okay. We women work as well as the men, that's not the point, but we do so with our own consciousness'.

As for consciousness, she has more than enough, does the valorous Christine. And you will gain a little more by tasting her wine. A true summer rosé, balanced and fresh, suave and delicate, more delicate than most Tavel rosés, with a pleasant hint of pink grapefruit as a finale, but also with everything that makes Tavel different to a rosé from elsewhere – delicious body and a dense texture. Marry it with a salad of prawns and citrus and or a carpaccio of raw home-marinated salmon.

Domaine de Tourtouil
Chemin des Comeyres
30126 Tavel
Tel.: +33 (0)4 66 50 05 68
E-mail: domainedetourtouil@orange.fr
Website: www.vin-rose-tavel.com

Château de Trinquevedel
THE CONTINUATION OF A HISTORY

Guillaume Demoulin

'The farmhouse dates from the eighteenth century and was built on the foundations of a building that dates back to the twelfth century, so the site is full of history. Famous people, the nobility and writers were the respective owners, one of whom, the Count of Rochefort, was even assassinated here during the Revolution. My great-grandfather acquired Trinquevedel in 1936. At Trinquevedel, we make virtually nothing but Tavel, something that is rather rare, and we blend it from six of the nine permitted vine stocks. Its specificity consists in the high proportion of Clairette in the blend, which gives it its very individual style. Furthermore, our vines are grown exclusively on the sandy terroir, the terroir that has given Tavel its reputation and which has made it distinctive through its minerality and its finesse. It was the first type of soil to be cultivated when viticulture began here. When combined with a white grape stock such as Clairette, it provides that spicy, aniseed note that is so easy to recognise in our wines. This happy combination is something I want to exploit to its maximum potential, as well as preserving it, by working in an environmentally friendly way so as to bequeath a healthy and sustainable terroir to my children. The château de Trinquevedel is one of the oldest wine-producing properties in the region. Through duty and through conviction, I want to continue this long history. The Tavel we make today is faithful to that which we produced six years ago and is barely different to what was being produced a hundred years ago. I want to produce traditional wines, made for matching with good food, and with ripe, fruity aromas. That is my only concession to modernity and to the consumer's expectations. Our wines remain true wines of the South, fine, spicy and dense, with notes of fruits and yellow flowers, supported by a hint of freshness. They should be drunk with white meat or spicy, Moroccan or Asian dishes'.

Guillaume is one of the younger generation of Tavel wine-makers. He has been in charge of the property since 2006. As he recommends, his balanced Tavel which has great finesse, select but deep, can be matched with a whole range of dishes from world cuisine. But we also appreciate it after it has been kept for a few years as a wine of meditation, to be drunk while sitting by the fire, for instance. With its topaz highlights, its bouquet of flowers and aromatic herbs, it would enhance a discussion between faithful friends of a fleeting memory of a distant summer evening. Since, despite its finesse, this Tavel has keeping qualities. I served a few well-chosen guests with a perfectly constituted 1989, with delicious notes of rancio. Success and surprise were assured.

Château de Trinquevedel
Trinquevedel
30126 Tavel
Tel.: +33 (0)4 66 50 04 04
E-mail: demoulin@chateau-trinquevedel.fr
Website: www.chateau-trinquevedel.fr

Seigneur de Vaucrose
IN PRAISE OF MATURITY

Jean Lévêque

'My ancestors, the Desmarais de Vaucrose, came down here from Normandy in 1500. They purchased the manor of Tavel from the Count of Rochefort. I am the last descendant of the lords of Tavel. Before World War II, my parents sold the harvest in bottles under the brand name of Clos de Vaucrose. Later, the wine was sold in bulk. In 1965, my brother and I decided to resume the sale in bottles, we did the research and found that in order to be allowed to use the name of 'Clos', our vineyard needed to be enclosed by a wall or surrounded by a hedge. Since this was not the case, we registered the trade mark of Seigneur de Vaucrose. In 2005, my brother withdrew from the property by selling his share of the vineyard so I bought 50% of the shares in the building. Our vineyard, situated on the clay-and-silica and clay-and-limestone terroirs is planted with Grenache, Cinsault, Carignan, Syrah, Mourvèdre, pink and white Clairette and a little Bourboulenc. We produce a classic Tavel, as complex as it is elegant. It is the colour of the wines made by my parents, for which we have an excellent description produced by a cousin of my father's who was a poetess. She speaks of a golden, pale ruby wine, shaded with topaz. We have remained faithful to this traditional colour of Tavel and to the wine that goes with it, a wine that benefits from aging even if, in future, we shall also be producing a slightly more fruity wine. But the customers come to me mainly to find what they cannot find elsewhere –Tavels of a certain age. So we continue to sell our Tavels between three and five, and even six years after they have been bottled. Old wines are wines that are no longer fit to drink. As for us, we sell our wines old, which is not the same thing. In 1973, I was burning the remains of some chemicals but I breathed in the gas and became very ill. This encouraged me to stop using chemicals other than copper and sulphur. So for the past few decades, I have been working organically although I do not have organic certification. We are currently in the process of conversion. We shall soon be given the label. At the time, I was a trail-blazer. Now, I'm just fashionable'.

A true lord of the manor, and Lord Jean's wine is just as aristocratic, an old-style Tavel with its colour, its topaz reflections, its finely spiced nose, it's mildness and smoothness. It is a wine full of gentleness, that does not impose and whose structure, that ensures its keeping qualities, are only revealed in the finale. Decant it into an elegant carafe and serve it with cold sea fish (preferably salmon or sea-bass) in aspic.

Seigneur de Vaucrose
Le Village
Route de Lirac
30126 Tavel
Tel.: +33 (0)4 66 50 04 37
Email: seigneurdevaucrose@orange.fr
Website: www.seigneurdevaucrose.com

Domaine Le Vieux Moulin
FOLLOWING THROUGH WITH IDEAS

Sébastien Jouffret

'As co-owner with my father, I represent the sixth generation at Le Vieux Moulin estate. In 2002, we created the current estate which was originally devoted to growing fruit trees. I had always wanted to make wine, and even when I was quite small I only set one condition for teaming up with my father – we must stop growing fruit trees. If my two grandfathers, one gave me a love of growing things and the other the pleasure of wine-making. Of course, the vinification technique, especially chilling and filtering, did not exist in the days of my maternal grandfather. So I had to learn them elsewhere. But my grandfather was always ready to taste the wines, and he still contributes his opinion about the blending. In 2002, the cellar was moved to the edge of the village, where we were able to enlarge and modernise the facilities. My grandfather claims that the wines rediscovered the style they had in the past with a lot of fruitiness, length, body and structure, true Tavel wines of which we are obviously very proud. For a few years, our wines were more general, without their own expression. Of course, most of the work was done in the vineyard. We work our soils, we are better able to select the varieties, but the cellar helps to create the wine that we want to produce. We work as a family, each being responsible for their own sector. My father manages the vineyard which currently covers 60 hectares, taking all the appellations together, of which five hectares are Tavel. My wife and my mother deal with the sales and the administrative side. My own kingdom is the cellar. Long before the harvest, we define the types of wine we wish to produce. Since 2008, we have been picking from three o'clock to eleven o'clock in the morning, that way we avoid chilling the grapes too much and are in better control of the vinification. What needs changing? Certainly not the label, it has lasted for six generations, it is known to the customers, it is part of our history and even that of the appellation. But we could modernise the taste, yes, the fruitiness, giving the wine more structure, more length, less alcohol. Most of our blends consist of Grenache and Cinsault, although we use almost all the varieties in the appellation, both red and white. To make a good Tavel, you need a perfectly mature grape which corresponds to a degree of alcohol that is become higher and higher with the very hot years that we are currently experiencing. Despite our know-how and our technique, we remain, above all, at the mercy of the weather'.

He follows his ideas through, does Sébastien. Despite his youth, he has acquired a solid reputation as an exceptional wine-maker, even those with a great reputation ask for his advice! His Tavel delights through its precision, cleanliness, its aromatic intensity, its structure and density as well as through its finely spicy notes of tropical fruits and its 'drinkability'. This is a contemporary Tavel, faithful to its origins that goes so well with any cuisine in the world. We chose it to accompany grilled kebabs marinated in spices and lime juice – totally delicious!

Famille Roudil - Jouffret
Domaine Le Vieux Moulin
Domaine Le Vieux Lavoir
Le Palai Nord -
Route de la Commanderie
30126 Tavel
Tel.: +33 (0)4 66 82 85 11
E-mail: roudil-jouffret@wanadoo.fr
Website: www.caveroudil.com

Domaine du Vieux Relais
THE ART OF SCULPTING THE VINE

Mireille Bastide

'We are here in an old post-house built in 1870. Travellers from Uzès who arrived on horseback or in wagons stopped here and left with full stomachs and fresh horses. It was bought by my great-grandparents who began growing grapes here. The vines occupy four very different types of soil – stony, sandy, clay and limestone. My wine derives all its character and strength from this. Since they all mature at different times, each terroir is harvested separately, later for the loam and clay soils, earlier for the limestone lauses where the vine can succumb quicker to drought. Nothing in the world would make me abandon any of the four terroirs. Each has their *raison d'être* and it is they that make my Tavel so typical. The fact that they are so scattered is a disadvantage, because I have to work on thirty-two different plots and although they are not far away from each other, I have to run around all over the place during the harvest, something that requires a lot of time and perseverance. This diversity, which means that each soil has to be worked differently, is thus an eternal challenge, but that is just what I enjoy in my job. Every year, before the harvest, I visit all my plots and assess how ripe the grapes are. Despite its being split up, the vineyard is not large, I can harvest quickly and that is how I avoid too high an alcohol content, which rarely exceeds an average of 13 degrees. The blending of the grapes from the various plots is performed gradually. I don't hurry anything. Apparently, I make a Tavel that is like me, a wine of character, spicy, developed but with flexibility.

I like to work on a small scale but well. That way, I can do most of the work on my own, whether on the tractor or in the cellar. If I had a little more time, I would do more landscaping work. I would like my vineyard to look like a little garden. I have a very close relationship with the plant. When I prune it, I talk to it and give the appropriate shape to each strain. It's my form of artistry'.

If you talk to her about plants, about living nature, about the garden and her eyes start to shine. And she will chat to you for ages about her experiences, her contact with the plant world. Her wine is full of character, both powerful and fresh, and it is thus a wine of nature, to be drunk in the open air, perhaps during a lavish picnic eaten in the shade of a venerable oak, beside a little stream which will cool the wine far better than any ice-bucket.
Not currently sold in bottles.

Domaine du Vieux Relais
Route de la Commanderie
30126 Tavel
Tel.: +33 (0)6 08 34 15 54
E-mail: mireillebastide@sfr.fr

Les vignerons de Tavel
UNITED AND VISIONARY

Paul Sanchez, directeur
Christian Paly, président

'Created and built 1937 by several early adopters and visionaries of the appellation, the Cellar of the Vignerons de Tavel was officially inaugurated on 31 July 1938 by the then President of the French Republic, Albert Lebrun himself. This is almost certainly the only cooperative in France to have been honoured in this way. When it was created, the cellar had a membership of about forty wine-makers who gathered together to improve the quality of their output, and to market and add value to their product. We started by making 3,000 hectolitres, and today we make more than 30,000 hectolitres. We have fifty active wine-makers, illustrating how the cellar has developed in recent decades. From its creation, the wine-makers were very united and shared the vision of their future and that of their children.

We remain a structure with a human face in which dialogue is still possible. Thus, future projects will be more achievable in terms of contemplation and orientation, culminating in decision-making. We shall therefore continue to improve the quality of our products and market them better, especially for export. In its human, cultural and economic aspects, the cellar has had an undeniable influence on the village, its environment, and even the landscape. It represents half the Tavel appellation and is a landmark at the entrance to the village, with its magnificent, early twentieth-century, neo-Provençal architecture, built of chiselled stone. Each successive generation of its member enlarged it, while respecting the image and aesthetic of this monument to the cooperative movement in the Rhone valley. We have nothing to "blush" about for being a cooperative cellar, we are proud of the fact. Our cellar is also a magnificent working tool that enables us to produce high quality rosés, because everything was designed, even in former times, to enable us to work using gravity. This means that the musts are never pumped. We follow the classic developments in œnology such as chilling the musts to preserve the maximum primary aromas, and we proceed to clarify them prior to fermentation, so as to be able to get the best out of the grape and the juice. We also produce Lirac, Côtes-du-Rhône and vins de pays. But most of what we make is Tavel wine. We vinify our three terroirs separately in order to preserve all their specificity'.

In terms of brand image, a cooperative cellar does not necessarily rank very high and often it has just one selling point – the quality of its wines. From the very first year when the cellar was in operation, in 1938, the price of Tavel increased. This will illustrate the correctness of the theory. Even today, the Tavel cellar is the best guarantee of the quality of most of the wines sold under the appellation. The people of Tavel are proud of their cellar and its importance – and they are right. In Tavel, there can be no better value-for-pleasure ratio than the Cuvée Royale, which you can uncork for any occasion.

Les Vignerons de Tavel
Route de la Commanderie
30126 Tavel
Tel.: +33 (0)4 66 50 03 57
E-mail: contact@cavedetavel.com
Website: www.cavedetavel.com

Domaine la Rocalière
Taking care of every detail

Séverine Lemoine
Mélanie Borrelly

'Our estate was founded in 1995, on the initiative of my father, my grandfather and my great-uncle. I had just completed my studies and I joined them so as to be able to take part in the adventure. Even though I have always been immersed in this environment, I was not predestined to work in a vineyard, but sometimes destiny takes over. When my father told me of his plan, I did not hesitate for long. I have always enjoyed challenges and taking over an estate of 50 hectares, 25 hectares of it in Tavel, was indeed quite a challenge! It meant dealing with the vinification, developing the marketing, creating a brand image – we weren't quite starting from scratch, but we were not far off.

I soon developed an enthusiasm for this world, and that is why I am still here today. For the past three years, I have been responsible for the entire estate. I am responsible main for the wine itself, while my sister Mélanie is in charge of marketing and administration.

From the outset, I was interested in the cellar, as well as the vinification which I soon took over completely. When my father retired, I also took an interest in grape-growing, something I knew little about. Today, I share my time between the vineyard and the cellar.

I am lucky enough to have some very nice terroirs that offer us multiple possibilities. The idea is to make something bespoke. In everything, I appreciate things that are well made, that fit exactly and that are balanced. I like what appears to be natural even if in reality it has involved a lot of hard work behind the scenes. Those who taste the fruits of my work ought merely to sense the pleasurable side of it.

I have high ideals when it comes to Tavel wine. I believe we have a terroir that deserves a lot of hard work and I try and deal with a whole host of details so that it can be expressed at its finest. It's hard to explain! For example, there are many ways of using a pump or harvesting a plot but there is often only one way that is perfectly suited to the case in point. It is not enough to say what needs to be done, you have to be there and monitor every operation carefully, everything needs to be supervised, everything has to be checked. Fifty hectares, is still on a human scale, one can exercise total control over the whole process. I did not want to acquire more vines, I just aim to do better.

I appreciate elegance in a wine, its controlled power. I am proud to present a product in which I can recognise myself, in which I have invested personally at every level. I do not like impostors, I look for truth, for what is right and good.

Since this summer, we have been converting to organic, which is absolutely part of the logic of our thorough way of working. In particular, working the soil enables us to reveal certain aromas to their advantage, the terroir can thus express itself even better. Organic cultivation is not really a constraint, all that is needed is a little more rigour and observation. In any case, I could not do it any other way. It's a question of wine-making philosophy and ethics. One cannot evoke the terroir without taking care of it, protecting it and preserving it'.

Séverine produces two cuvées of Tavel, a blend from the three terroirs in the classic style that is delicious and fresh, and the pearl of the estate's crop, a more mineral Tavel with a stronger personality that combines power and elegance. These two particularly carefully made products are redolent of a love of work well done, with care being taken over the slightest detail, something of which Séverine is so proud. You should choose the first cuvée for drinking as an aperitive or to eat with a dish based on vegetables. As for the second, it should ideally accompany grilled meat, such as lamb cutlets coated with some black tapenade.

Domaine la Rocalière
Le Palai Nord
Route de la Commanderie
30126 Tavel
Tel.: +33 (0)4 66 50 12 60
Email: rocaliere@wanadoo.fr
Website: www.domainelarocaliere.com

Savouring and Cooking

Any self-respecting wine should be drunk with food, and Tavel is no exception to the rule. Let us remember its advantages for one final time. They are those of a great, ambitious, complex wine with a rare and unique balance, that combines the advantages of a white wine and those of a red wine, but knows how to circumvent their disadvantages. Tavel has few enemies in the food world and is rarely in danger of being mismatched. On the contrary, it is often the only wine that can be drunk without a problem with food or dishes that are hard to match with wine, such as artichokes, gazpacho, an omelette or salmon.

Tavel is complex but not complicated and is thus the ideal companion to a healthy cuisine full of freshness. We could marry it with tomato in all its cooked forms, with casseroled broad beans, flavoured with a little garlic and a few mint leaves, a slice of lightly grilled country ham, a ratatouille, slices of aubergine, courgette or sweet pepper brushed with oil and grilled over a wood fire accompanied by a soft cheese spiced up with a little harissa, pistou or mixed herbs. Tavel wine ennobles so many unusual flavours such as sweet-and-salt or acid-and-bitter and goes wonderfully with world cuisines, such as that of the Pacific Rim. It finds inspiration from the culinary culture of North Africa, China, Mexico or India, with a variety of dishes ranging from a tagine of couscous, jambalaya, paella, from a Reunion 'cari' to an Indian curry, from a samosa to salt cod croquettes, from wonton to spring rolls.

Tavel combines just as happily with fresh noodles, pizza, antipasti, tapas, a potato omelette, a Spanish tortilla, chile con carne, a whole baked salmon or salmon steaks, grilled, marinated or smoked, a beef carpaccio or scallops, cold roast beef accompanied by a rocket salad and with *vitello tonnato*, an Italian recipe consisting of cold cooked veal thinly sliced and coated with a light mayonnaise sauce, served with tuna and capers.

Not fearing a mixture of food types, its aromas and its smooth texture will enhance any menu, from a simple melon with raw ham to goat's cheese with herbs, via a grilled sea-bass on a bed of wild fennel or a rack of lamb with Provençal herbs.

Tavel proves just as happy a marriage with classic French cuisine, even dishes that are a little old-fashioned. It goes very well with a gratin of crayfish tails, chicken or turkey à la cordon bleu, stuffed breast of veal, duck with orange, rabbit with prunes, duck confit, Christmas turkey with chestnut stuffing, pheasant terrine, roast wild boar, a classic Alsatian *choucroute*, a roast Bresse chicken *demi-deuil* (meaning with slices of black truffle placed under the skin).

Tavel happily combines with simpler dishes but which are just as delicious such as a spicy grilled sausage with Espelette pimento or with herbs, a Troyes *andouillette* (tripe sausage) of the finest quality, a calf's head in *sauce gribiche*, a pork hock served on a bed of green beans, breaded sheep's feet, grilled calves' liver with fried onions, a slice of ham cooked on the bone and served warm, a rice or potato salad.

Tavel can also be the Prince Charming to accompany creative and inspired cuisine in which experimentation and improvisation predominate. Tavel will enhance monkfish with bacon lardons and cherry tomato, veal sweetbreads with ceps and morels, lobster salad with citrus, roast partridge served on a bed of green cabbage conservatively cooked like spinach or honey-roast pigeon or quail, accompanied by spring turnips and chervil with salted butter.

Through its great richness, high concentration and very complex balance, there is only one thing that it refuses to grant the sophisticated gourmets that we are, namely, its use as an ingredient in a dish such as, for example, using it in marinades, gravies or sauces.

But perhaps the picky sermonising of a sommelier with a considerable reputation irritates you somewhat, or the professorial discourse of a connoisseur will make you more inebriated than the wine you will be served. All you want is to drink a good bottle to go with a perfect dish, without getting a good conduct medial as a wine-loving gastronome. In such a case, Tavel is just what you need. For your satisfaction, choose any bottle at any time of year from any producer and in any year for any dish and you are already assure of success and infallible pleasure.

But if you are eager to join in this sport that consists of the best combination of food and wine, testing the most surprising combinations and the most complementary flavours, Tavel will enable you to explore in greater depth and detail its multiple gustatory depths. Before doing so, you will have taken care to stock your cellar with the wines of several wine-makers who vinify in different styles. This will provide you with a first-rate palette adapted to the most varied and infinite nuances. Do not hesitate to place them in the darkest corner of your cellar to allow the wine to age, by forgetting some of your valuable bottles for five, ten, even twenty years. Once this period is over, you will be surprised to discover new flavours that you were not aware of in them. Finally, here are a few choice proposals to create successful combinations:

- Fruity Tavels bottled in the year following the harvest should preferably be drunk as an aperitive, with tapas, light dishes, vegetables that have been lightly boiled to remain crunchy or goat's cheese.

- Fiery, classic Tavels, powerful and well structure, can be drunk throughout the meal, with grilled chicken, veal, or organic pork, or with pizza, pasta and hard, fruity cheeses.

- Chastened Tavels, aged between eighteen months and three years, go well with almost anything, but especially with vegetables, dishes that are typical of southern France and classic French cuisine.

- The elegant and balanced Tavels that are mineral and finely spiced will be chosen to accompany creative, inspired, modern and light cuisine, using the finest quality ingredients.

- Aged Tavels, five, ten or even twenty years old, with rancio aromas similar to those of an old tawny port, and a silky structure like that of the Portuguese drink, but minus the residual sugar, go well with rather unusual dishes with very special flavours. This could be pasta sprinkled with parsley and eaten with mature cheeses such as Bleu de Gex, Fourme d'Ambert or Stilton, or those that are even more aged such as Mimolette vieille, an old Swiss Emmental, an aged Salers, Comté that is 24 months old or even a dish such as duck with orange, foie gras with crystallised fruits, chicken with morels, a pear and Roquefort tart. All these go wonderfully with aged Tavel.

TOURING AND ACCOMMODATION

Tavel is the perfect place starting-point for exploring the département of Gard, Languedoc-Roussillon or Provence. Sheltered from the turbulence of a noisy, agitated world, by the safety tapes of the autoroute and the TGV train line, Tavel nestles at the foot of its secret little valley a stone's throw from the deafening reality of Greater Avignon, not far from the cities of art and performances – Arles and Nîmes.

But do not expect to find a sophisticated setting consisting of the latest tourist infrastructure. Despite the mayor of Tavethes stated purpose of promoting the commune in the near future to a centre of high-quality wine tourism, Tavel remains a rather sleepy little village but with good roads thanks to the départementale arterial road that runs through it, cutting it in half. The road is lined with a few cellars that are happy to welcome wine-lovers, a three-star inn and de three or four high-quality café-restaurants – though these are often closed at night, an ironmonger's and two bakeries fragrant in the early morning with pure-butter croissants and crunchy baguettes.

To visit the unique Saint-Vincent cellar, the only true tourist institution in the village, you will need to manage to wedge yourself into one of the rare parking spots. The wine shop is competently managed by Sylvie Tribert, a Grand Master of the Commanderie and imperious ambassadress for Tavel, who will inculcate you with the knowledge of a connoisseur, supported by tastings, into the subtle differences between the wines of the cru. Then, having once again negotiated the traffic which never lets up, in order perilously bring back a few bottles to your car, you will leave Tavel without any regrets, satisfied to be safe and sound, the car boot filled with the eighth wonder of the world.

You will then tell yourself that there is not much to do in Tavel and you will barely retain a distant memory, possibly refreshed by the wine you will subsequently uncork. But do not judge by appearances. The village only reveals its true self to the visitor willing to spend a few night there. You will be received with open arms by beaming hosts, even during the summer season, at the Auberge de Tavel or the numerous guesthouses run by the locals which are increasing in number.

Like a cat that gradually explores its new territory by making wider and wider concentric circles, you will set out to explore this charming village. After leaving the busy, noisy, but reassuring main street, you will gradually penetrate the narrow alleys in which you will find shady paths edged with hollyhocks, nasturtiums and morning glory, carefully tended by a loving gardener. You will walk beside Tavethes stone walls at the foot of which wind tiny streams that feed a picturesque communal laundry. You will admire the exceptional gardens of artisans in which fig-trees and cherry-trees flourish beside tomato plants and pyramids of runner beans or the last Tavel coco-beans that descend in a cascade of greenery.

Then, preferably on foot or on a bicycle, you will take the road to the vineyards, carrying a basket of delicious local produce. You will stop in the centre of a landscape of immaculate white stones glistening in the sun, sprinkled

with a few ancient vines whose branches sway in the wind, loaded with just a few bunches of grapes. Once you have sat down in the shade of a knotty umbrella pine or venerable holm-oak, you will be able to eat your picnic and taste a great wine of the cru.

Only the next day, or even the day after that, will you venture a little further. Only a few kilometres separate you from exploring Avignon, city of the popes and the famous Saint-Bénézet bridge, the tower of Philippe-the-Bel or the Fort Saint-André at Villeneuve-lès-Avignon, an ancient sentinel guarding the breath-taking panorama of the Mont Ventoux in the Alpilles. You may even push on later as far as Orange or Châteauneuf-du-Pape, you may contemplate the amazing Pont du Gard, an amazing Roman aqueduct on three levels that brought water from the spring at Eure, at the foot of Uzès, to the Roman city of Nemausus, now known as Nîmes. You will visit Nîmes which still retains remarkable monuments such as the arenas, the Maison Carrée and the Tour Magne. This rich ancient past has given the city the nickname

of 'French Rome'. You will travel through the Camargue, the villages of Saintes-Maries-de-the-Mer, Arles, the Luberon, Saint-Rémy-de-Provence and the many other treasures of the region. Every evening, you will return to the cool and calm of the village of Tavel, you will remember the delightful cultural sights you witnessed during the day. These might include the street theatre and plays at the Avignon Festival or the photo exhibitions of the International Encounters at Arles. Naturally, culinary pleasures are very much on the menu of your discoveries. These might include the olive oil press in the Vaucluse or in the Vallée des Beaux, the big street-markets in the towns of the region, where stalls display goat's cheese, honey, local charcuterie and many other mouth-watering produce from the local farms. You will not hesitate to take home many of these goodies to prolong your pleasure. As for the wines, there is an embarrassment of choice. The people of Tavel, who are good neighbours, will pardon your curiosity and your visits to the local wine-makers of Lirac, Costières-de-Nîmes or Côtes-du-Rhône. Tavel, lying at the confluence of the Rhône Valley, Provence and Languedoc, will thus not only have offered you hospitality and most exceptional wines but also the possibility, from a reserved and reassuring base camp, to discover a region that is overflowing with cultural, culinary and sight-seeing treasures in an abundance that is envied throughout the world.

A PLACE TO STAY

Auberge de Tavel***
Voie romaine - 30126 Tavel
Tel: +33 (0)4 66 50 03 41
Fax: +33 (0)4 66 50 24 44
aubergedetavel@yahoo.fr
www.auberge-de-tavel.com

Jardin de Bacchus
A quality guesthouse
High Standard B & B
Rue de Tourtouil - 30126 Tavel
Tel: + 33 (0)4 66 90 28 62
jardindebacchus@free.fr
http://jardindebacchus.fr

Les Chambres de Vincent
B & B and Gite
Rues des Grillons - 30126 Tavel
Tel: +33(0)6 12 05 75 56 et +33(0)4 66 50 94 76
nancy@chambres-de-vincent.com
www.chambres-de-vincent.com

Élisabeth & Philippe Cirillo
Guesthouse in the village
Rue des grillons - 30126 Tavel
Tel: +33 (0)4 66 50 34 10 / +33 (0)6 72 37 58 91

L'Hostellerie du Seigneur
Guesthouse
Mme Bodo Juliette
Place du Seigneur - 30126 Tavel
Tel: +33 (0)4 66 50 04 26

L'enclos de l'Olivier
Guesthouse
Gilberte Thouverez
Chemin des Oliviers - 33126 Tavel
Tel: +33 (0)4 66 50 03 20

Mireille Mazzoleni
Self-catering in adjoining chalets deep in the
countryside.
Three Stars
Les Griottes
Route Romaine - 30126 Tavel
Tel: +33 (0)4 66 50 04 64
Fax: +33 (0)4 66 50 04 64
www.les-griottes-tavel.fr

PLACES TO EAT

Auberge de Tavel***
Voie romaine - 30126 Tavel
Tel: +33 (0)4 66 50 03 41
Fax: +33 (0)4 66 50 24 44
aubergedetavel@yahoo.fr
www.auberge-de-tavel.com

Restaurant Le Physalis (centre du village)
Rue Frédéric Mistral - 30126 Tavel
Tel: +33 (0)4 66 50 29 53

Restaurant La Genestière
Chemin de Cravailleux - 30126 Tavel
Tel: +33 (0)4 66 50 94 56
Fax: +33 (0)4 66 50 98 22
genestiere@wanadoo.fr
www.genestiere.com

Bar/Restaurant La Tablée
Rue Frédéric Mistral - 30126 Tavel
Tel: +33 (0)4 66 50 06 21

Bar/Restaurant Au Bon Accueil
Rue Frédéric Mistral - 30126 Tavel
Tel: +33 (0)4 66 33 05 49

PLACE TO SHOP

Caveau Saint Vincent
Sylvie Tribert
Place du Seigneur - 30126 Tavel
Tel: +33 (0)4 66 50 24 10
Fax: +33 (0)4 66 50 43 33
saint.vincent.tavel@laposte.net

Contents

Book Design: Walid Salem, Perfecto

Monitoring: Perfecto, Bordeaux, France

Printed in Italy, November 15, 2011
Legal Deposit in November 2011